Femdom

The Erotic Guide to Female Domination

Marisa Rudder

Marisa Rudder

Author of *12 Books in the Best-Selling Love & Obey Female led Relationship*

Available on Amazon Books

Please contact: Marisa Rudder

Email: femaleledrelationshipbook@gmail.com

Printed in the United States of America Publisher's Cataloging-in-Publication data

ISBN: 978-1-7361835-6-4

DEDICATION

I would like to dedicate this book to all the strong, brave ladies who have joined or about to join the *Love & Obey* movement and live a female led lifestyle and the supportive gentlemen who recognized the natural superiority of females. It is also my desire that women and men experience the joy, happiness, and passion from exploring all aspects of a loving Female Led Relationship (FLR) and understanding all the benefits of a loving female authority. If you have not already, please join us on social media. You can find out more at our website:

www.loveandobey.com

Or follow me on social media:

FACEBOOK
https://www.facebook.com/femaleledrelationships

TWITTER
https://twitter.com/loveandobeybook

INSTAGRAM
https://www.instagram.com/femaleledrelationships

Introduction

Imagine a world where your Queen throws you down and gets on top of you, pinning down your hands, and restraining your hips with her thighs. Or better yet, she blindfolds you, undresses you, and teases you with her whip. Perhaps she has you tied up naked, wearing a chastity cage, unable to move or say a word. The sight of a leather-clad, dominant, sexy Queen shouting orders or being in control of you is irresistible. Not to mention, all of the fun, exciting ideas you can add to transform your sex life. Why is the fantasy of Femdom so exciting? Men and women have admitted to being obsessed with engaging in domination and submission. More couples are admitting to being interested in female domination and adding it to their daily lives.

Femdom, or female dominance, is a BDSM activity in which the Queen is in charge. BDSM is a variety of erotic practices involving bondage discipline dominance and submission sadomasochism. BDSM involves one partner being submissive and the other being dominant. Femdom involves the Queen being the dominant and taking control while her man is the submissive and submits to her. Femdom is the more intense version of a Female Led Relationship (FLR). Most couples start out in FLR with moderate aspects of female domination, such as the Queen taking charge of the household, making the major decisions, giving the orders, and being in control in the bedroom.

Female Led Relationships are much more focused on day-to-day interactions where the Queen is in charge in the relationship and her man serves her as the supportive gentleman. However, after some time in an FLR, many couples want to increase the intensity of domination and submission, especially in the bedroom. Men often like Femdom as a means to escape being in charge and as a sincere way to show their devotion and worship of their Queen. Couples want to add some aspects of light BDSM to spice up their sex life and it leads to some very interesting and adventurous lovemaking. Men become obsessed and many of them need to feel fully under their woman's control.

Femdom is the next step, and it's all about the Queen's ability to trigger your hidden desires and fears with her domination of you. What turns you on? Is it the sensation of your wrists, ankles, and body getting restrained with ropes in bondage? Or is it the touch of a whip moving along your legs and buttocks? Or perhaps the sting of a paddle or being blindfolded and teased? The look on Michael Douglas's face in *Basic Instinct* when Sharon Stone's character, Catherine Tramell, is straddled over him as she pulls out a silk scarf and ties his hands to bedposts is probably a scene you'd want to recreate. The sheer terror mixed with excitement and sexual arousal was so exhilarating to watch that it gives you a taste of how this will feel when you experience it. This is the power of Femdom in your sex life.

There is a reason Femdom has exploded with over 823,000 searches monthly on Google. There is no doubt that an interest in female dominance is growing as more women are stepping into their roles as powerful Queens and men are obsessed with feeling their power and control over them. Dominance and submission are already happening at home and at work. More women occupy positions of power, and many men are becoming more accustomed to taking direction from a woman in control. Now, couples are adopting the female led lifestyle structure at home and in the bedroom.

In a Female Led Relationship, the desire to be controlled daily by a strong female becomes even more important. More women are taking control in many aspects of their lives, and many are leading countries, governments, corporations, cities, households, and now the bedroom. My previous books *Love & Obey* and *Queendom* are blockbuster hits and provide the essential guidance that a couple needs to build a lasting, successful relationship. Part of keeping the spark alive in all relationships is to add domination and discipline.

One of the other reasons Femdom becomes imperative today is because it reinforces the idea of female superiority and smashes the patriarchy. Queens can now take the responsibility of training men to transition from patriarchal to supportive gentleman, first through basic FLR to the next level which is Femdom.

If you want to take your Female Led Relationship or marriage to a new level of excitement and adventure, then Femdom could be for you. Fifty percent of marriages end in divorce and at least 25 percent of relationships are on the brink of breaking up. Something needs to change. I believe that switching to a Female Led Relationship or female led marriage is the key. I have received nothing but glowing messages of appreciation for how this lifestyle has completely saved marriages and relationships.

A staggering 70 percent of divorces are initiated by women, which means that they are driven to the point of no return, beginning with lack of proper service and attention from their men, a breakdown in communication, and contrasting goals. However, I believe the biggest issue is a lack of sexual fulfillment. If all this changes, what would life be like? In Female Led Relationships, the man is focused on his woman and worships her like the Queen she is. Sex is for the Queen first, and her pleasure is priority. Now take it a step further with Femdom. A Queen who steps into her role as a leader while her man is the submissive, supportive gentleman changes a lack of attention to an inward focus on the relationship or marriage. Both you and your Queen are sexually fulfilled, and the relationship or marriage is exciting and filled with all kinds of adventures.

Femdom is for those couples who want to increase the intensity of domination and submission in their daily lives and sex lives. Femdom is not for everyone, and if you are new to a female led lifestyle, you may want to begin at the Female Led Relationship level. However, if you are ready to experience a life that is sexually charged, exciting, and filled with thrilling, unpredictable adventures, then everything I describe about Femdom could be for you. I hope couples who are in Female Led Relationships and already experiencing the happiness and fulfillment from such a lifestyle will gain even more satisfaction from Femdom.

Femdom is the next step for your FLR if you want a more intense experience. If you want to make things more extreme, yet create a deeper, more fulfilling, and sexually arousing, then learning and practicing all aspects of Femdom is the key.

x

Table of Contents

CHAPTER 1
What is Femdom?

Femdom is exploding in 2022, and more couples are interested in this type of experience than ever before. Women are aware of their power as Queens in society, and if you enjoy Female Led Relationships and you want to take things to a whole new level of intensity, then Femdom could be for you. Femdom simply means female dominance and will dramatically transform any normal vanilla relationship into daily exciting adventures. It's fitting today because so many women enjoy their new role as the dominant in their relationships. In fact, female dominance appeals to men and women today since men have become obsessed with dominant, take-charge Queens and women desire to be a "badass."

Femdom originates in the BDSM (bondage, discipline, sadism, and masochism) community, in which a dominant takes charge during consensual sex acts involving power, pain, or humiliation, and the submissive is the person who submits. In Femdom, the dominant is the woman while the man is submissive, and he enthusiastically accepts his role as servant, submissive, and subservient. Femdom provides a framework for the relationship, yet it offers so many opportunities to explore sexually.

Women get to step into their power as Queens and ultimate ruler, and men can worship and enjoy a powerful woman having complete control over them. You and your Queen will witness a transformation in your relationship or marriage with Femdom because it is female focused. You will experience more love and devotion as both of your needs are fulfilled. Femdom is intended for those couples who are already in a Female Led Relationship and want to increase the intensity of their experience. However, many vanilla couples will also choose to add Femdom to spice things up or as part of sexploration.

Femdom often begins in a man's mind as fantasy, but I feel that men have a deep-seated desire for female authority stemming from their relationships with their mothers. For many of their development years, a man's mother was a powerful authority figure, with whom he forms a lifelong bond, which is why the saying "men marry their mothers." Men will often seek a Queen who embodies similar characteristics as their mothers. The desire for female authority and Femdom begins in a man's formative years. The interaction with his mother is the first real experience a man has with female authority, and I believe he never forgets it. In fact, he craves it.

When men are finally working and living in the modern world, he encounters numerous examples of female authority in his bosses, co-workers, and dates, particularly in professional fields. More women occupy positions of power and men's desire for female dominance is triggered daily. This combined with porn and internet images and videos increases his desire for dominance. Men will tend to act out their fantasies about Femdom, first, with dominatrixes or they learn about it online.

Sometimes this is their first real experience with Femdom. At times this may be exactly what they were looking for, but often it falls short of their expectations because what they really desire is a true Queen they can love and serve and can still fulfill their Femdom fantasies. It is my belief that men are searching for Queens who can be their ultimate master and ruler and can give them the daily dominating experience they crave.

My first books *Love & Obey* and *Real Men Worship Women* as well as *Queendom* dealt more with loving female authority and the creation of a successful Female Led Relationship. Now, we will explore the next level of female dominance in relationships in Femdom. We will discover how to make your female worship and servitude more intense but continue to experience all of the love, happiness, and excitement of an FLR. Adding aspects of Femdom to your relationship doesn't mean you're in a dungeon and participating in BDSM every day. But understanding the deeper fundamentals of Femdom and incorporating them into your relationship can dramatically transform your relationship or marriage. What men must realize, though, is that it is important to understand their Queens' desires and how they can serve her are the major goals in Femdom.

The most imperative rule to remember is that Femdom should always be explored in a safe and consensual way hence the Safe Sane Consensual (SSC) principle in which everything is based on safety and consensual activities, meaning both of you give your consent and are of sound mind and sane. Femdom should always be practiced in stages, so you start light then become more extreme if you both desire.

Femdom and the exploration of female domination in your relationship or marriage is sure to increase the intensity and transform your bond.

CHAPTER 2
Femdom and the Female Led Relationship

emdom and the Female Led Relationship requires trust and builds a deeper connection between you and your Queen, which is what makes them so powerful. A relationship or marriage based on trust lasts longer and remains stronger. Trust is what bonds you and your Queen for life. Femdom requires a great deal of honesty. When a man trusts his Queen enough to be honest about his deepest, most hidden desires, the relationship becomes more intimate and meaningful. When couples must keep their desires a secret, this eventually leads to deception, lies, dishonesty, and infidelity.

The man who trusts his Queen enough to submit his entire being to her needs will bond with her on a level that few men have experienced. Likewise, when a wife is powerful enough to rule her husband in love and daily life, this creates a much stronger and deeper connection in a way that most traditional marriages cannot offer.

To these couples, female domination is more than sexual. It is also social, emotional, and spiritual. In normal marriages, I feel that a lot remains hidden. Couples can go years never being free to express and show who they truly are. This facade can only be maintained for so long, and pretty soon, the truth is revealed, which can often lead to infidelity and break of trust. Contrast that with Femdom and female led life, deep desires are often shared, and communication tends to be better since discussion and daily communication is necessary in FLR. When your Queen is taking an active role in what happens daily, and you are devoted to serving her, the focus is always on the relationship, which is what makes female domination so much more appealing to modern men.

February 22, 2022, was a landmark day for the US women's soccer team for winning a major lawsuit victory for equal pay. Not only was this a win for women's sports, but it signified another giant step for women by finally gaining the respect and compensation for their work that they deserve. Women are beginning to be a dominant force in the workplace, and this dominance and power extends to the household.

Queens are taking charge of the bedroom and sex. But once Queens feel their power and control over men in the bedroom, they begin to express this sense of superiority in daily life. Female Led Relationships and Femdom are the beginning of the transformation, which occurs in the household where the Queens take charge and by feeling their power at home, they adopt this attitude in public. I feel this is one of the ways women feel more comfortable exerting their dominance and breaking barriers. We have seen more examples of women breaking through barriers in many industries in the last five years than any other time in history.

The media continually portray strong female characters in movies and TV shows, and social media is overflowing with strong Queens thriving. Femdom will help push Female Led Relationships into the forefront because it is essentially what both men and women desire.

Female Led Relationships have the power to transform lives. Each day is a new opportunity to explore the power dynamic of the Queen and submissive supportive gentleman. Femdom helps Queens to take this power dynamic to a whole new level. Whereas Female Led Relationships usually deal with the day-to-day activities of the Queen being in control and inserting aspects of Femdom, especially in the bedroom, which helps make life much more exciting and sexually arousing. Female led is a two-way street. Men desire a strong force in their Queens. It takes a submissive man to serve and encourage the Queen to step into her power. This helps the dominant Queen's personality to emerge. When a woman recognizes a man is in service to her and her wishes, she naturally begins to feel her superiority and she enjoys taking charge.

Femdom becomes an extremely powerful act in a Female Led Relationship. Here, the Queen is the ruler, and the man follows. Femdom represents a new opportunity for both men and women to explore their needs further and make things more intense and exciting. Men in Female Led Relationships want to submit. Since anything done in Femdom like spanking or other BDSM activities are only performed with consent, it means that only if the man is willing should the couple explore it. Therefore, it gives men the opportunity to learn to submit and empowers the Queen to have control, but both of you are gaining what you need out of the interaction.

Contrast this with a vanilla relationship where generally the man is in charge and the woman is left to be a servant to him and usually left sexually unfulfilled. By transitioning to Femdom and FLR, men, who are so accustomed to having all the power, are free to explore being led and serving a Queen. Most Queens would love to have a man who loves, honors, worships, and obeys her. The biggest dream of young girls is the Prince and Princess fantasy from stories like Cinderella. Girls are taught to believe that a man will come along, sweep them off their feet, and treat her like the most special person in the world.

Honestly, what woman wouldn't want a man who focuses his energy and his attention on her all of the time? A man who would cater to her every whim? Pamper her, give her foot and body massages, sexually satisfy her first? And who would get more pleasure out of pleasuring her than receiving pleasure himself? How about a man that would obey her every command and do whatever she told him to do, without arguing or complaining? A man who would not only do all of his chores, like taking care of the kids, doing the housework, laundry, grocery shopping, and even the cooking. How about a man who would wine and dine her and shower her with gifts? Unfortunately, this never happens in a vanilla relationship. But in a Female Led Relationship, this fantasy can come true and men are eager to do it.

FLR couples will use the idea of discipline from Femdom as the way in which the Queen disciplines the man for his transgressions or disobedience. If the Queen feels disrespected, she can suggest ten lashes during the spanking session in bed. For a more serious offense, such as getting drunk and not fulfilling his basic responsibility to maintain the home in a reasonable state of cleanliness, he might be in a time-out corner for a good half hour or have his privileges revoked. The Queen can resort to any number of activities for punishment, so in this way, FLR and Femdom overlap.

Both the Queen and her man must agree on the Femdom activities in which they will engage in because consent is still needed.

In FLR, once you start adding Femdom to your lifestyle, it becomes an exhilarating sexual fantasy, which will boost your lovemaking. Lots of dominant women do embrace wearing leather and add lots of BDSM activities as they provide great tools in the training and the disciplining of her man, as well as adding fun and excitement to their sex lives. Other women enjoy a softer version of domination and submission without all the formality. How you and your Queen decide to incorporate Femdom is your choice as long as you are both in agreement and constantly communicate.

CHAPTER 3
Why Men Love Strong Women and Discipline

Men love strong women, which is why Femdom is exploding. I believe they also crave discipline. Today, women are now freer to assert their dominance over men. Furthermore, many men welcome discipline from their Queens. Strong women are perceived as thrilling and anything can happen. Bad girls are the ones who will throw a man down, tie him up, strip off his pants, and tease him until he can't stand it anymore.

Who can resist giving up all of the power to a sexy, dominant woman fully capable of taking charge? Also, an unstable hierarchy can cause men considerable anxiety, whereas an established chain of command, such as those practiced by the military and many workplaces, works. When a man knows his Queen is in charge and agrees, he will be calmer and easier to deal with. There are fewer power struggles, arguments, and displays of ego, and aggressive outbursts.

In *Psychology Today*, after looking into the mating preferences of more than 5,000 men and women through a survey, researcher and biological anthropologist Helen Fisher, Ph.D., writes that men desire smart, strong, successful women. Her article showed that 87 percent of men said they would date a woman who was more intellectual than they were, better educated, and earned considerably more money than they did, while 86 percent claimed they were searching for a confident and self-assured woman.

Strong women go after the things they want in life. They don't sit by and wait for love to fall into their lap. They're not afraid to flirt and show a true interest, but they also define what they want in a relationship. They let a man know right away if they're looking for a simple hookup or if they're after a real relationship, and they don't stick around if a guy wants something different. Men don't have to guess with strong women, and they can sit back and let her make the first move and take control. This is the opposite of most other areas of life in which men must compete. With a woman in charge, they are free to allow her to lead and make decisions. This also makes the woman happier, and a happier woman is a much sexier woman.

Given the enormous variability in activities that people find arousing, there is no one way to be sexual. Men are especially stimulated by visual imagery, and about 90 percent report using pornography with some regularity, sometimes because they lack a partner or don't know how to bridge the differences in sexual appetite. Other reasons include interest that can occur between partners in the absence of discussing their sexual pleasures and sometimes for convenience.

Many people engage in behaviors once perceived as atypical, such as dominance play and anal intercourse. Researchers know that flexibility in sexual repertoires is healthy and generally enhances relationships. They also regard a specific behavior as problematic only when it creates harm or distress for one or both partners and when the behavior is compulsive.

Today, men are exploring submission, particularly in a Female Led Relationship, and the one thing that they all discover above anything else is that male submission to a strong Queen brings harmony to a home. There is no longer a power struggle between two people who both want to be "in charge." It is a confession of our dependence on one another and an acceptance of our natural roles—the woman as the leader and the Queen, and the man as her obedient and loyal subject.

Do you submit to your boss? If you are given instructions, do you follow them? If you don't, you would face discipline, wouldn't you? Your Queen is the "boss" of your home, and you must obey her or face discipline and other forms of punishment. Many patriarchal men see submission as a form of weakness or femininity. But in fact, it is much more of a form of chivalry, like the code of the knights serving a queen. So, when a man serves his wife or girlfriend, it's not out of weakness, but out of strength. A queen may discipline a disobedient knight so that he learns real men serve their superior woman. Discipline is necessary to remind men of their role and men should embrace the loving and caring spanking, paddling, caning, and whipping from their Queen.

Men in Female Led Relationships are looking for strong women who can consistently keep them in line and take control. Consistency makes a man form good habits and he feels he has been justly disciplined when he is spanked for misbehavior or disobedience. He understands that discipline and punishment is part of a consistent and fair system of FLR rules and consequences. Femdom rules should outline which behaviors are acceptable and the consequences dictate what kinds of punishment are necessary for breaking the rules. The justness of a discipline is not always the most crucial issue when it comes to female led discipline. A man will still gain great emotional and moral benefit from all discipline and training. It will still be useful and effective in the context of a Female Led Relationship.

One important reason why a man needs consistency in a Female Led Relationship is because it helps to remind him who is in charge. If he ever forgets, consistent discipline will teach him that his Queen is his supreme leader. Femdom is particularly effective in encouraging the Queen to step into her power and you are reminded that your purpose in life is to serve your Queen.

A consistent approach to disciplining a man for misbehavior is critical for maintaining his respect and love for the most important person in his life and it reinforces the woman's role as the leader of their relationship and household. If a man has been well-behaved for some time, then he can easily forget his responsibilities to himself and to his Queen. Forgetting his woman is also his Queen can lead him into temptation and increase the likelihood of masculine misbehavior. Consistent discipline will quickly and effectively resolve this problem.

Aggression is a complex social behavior with many causes and manifestations. Aggression can be physical or verbal.

Men can misinterpret aggressive women as too much of a challenge to handle, but in many cases, if they are in a loving relationship, a man can respond very well to aggressive women. For example, in spanking, the woman does the act — an activity showing aggression — if there is consent and the man wants it, the aggressive woman can be a major turn on, which can be very attractive to men.

Males generally have higher testosterone levels and are more aggressive than females. Similarly, because men are more violent and possess much higher testosterone concentrations than women, researchers suspected that testosterone is a strong cause of aggression in men. However, much less research has investigated this possibility in women. One study found that testosterone levels correlated with aggressive dominance. Although aggression and testosterone may be lower in women than men, many studies observed the same positive relationships between testosterone and aggression in women as they do in men. This means that men find strong, confident and aggressive women interesting because they show very similar traits to strong, confident men. A man can relate to the power of an assertive woman and respect her as his Queen. Through Femdom, you may witness aggression in your Queen, and as long as both agree on everything, this display of power and dominance will be sexually arousing.

Femdom activities have the power to deepen the bond between you and your Queen because there is love, honor, and respect.

CHAPTER 4
What is BDSM?

B DSM means bondage, discipline, sadism, and masochism and incorporates all sorts of activities that deal with a power exchange between domination and submission. Bondage is the sexual practice of tying up or restraining a partner. Discipline is defined as having power or influence over somebody and training them to obey rules, often using punishment to correct disobedience. Sadism is deriving pleasure from receiving pain or punishment, and masochism is deriving pleasure from inflicting pain or humiliation.

The D/S is also used to describe a Dominant/Submissive relationship. There are different aspects to BDSM, but Femdom falls into the area of power exchange where you, the submissive, is giving power to the dominant, your Queen, and she is receiving power from you. This constitutes the exchange.

Femdom uses aspects of BDSM when performed with the Queen, which involves leading and taking charge in the dominant position. When people think of Femdom, though, they believe it only involves a dominatrix. Many women are initially against the idea of Femdom because they are unsure if they want to get into the role of a dominatrix. But a dominatrix is a professional who is paid to be dominant and partake in BDSM activities with clients. Femdom in relationships are much different since it is based on free will, consent, and daily life. How much you want Femdom life to infiltrate daily life are some aspects to think about. Will you dabble in Femdom only in the bedroom or will it transfer to daily activities? The great thing about Femdom is the ability to explore it at any level.

A successful BDSM relationship is a power exchange, and you must lay the foundation. BDSM is all about control. Some people enjoy exerting control where others find joy in surrendering themselves to a dominant partner. Practicing BDSM sex in a relationship can be enjoyable as it will be a form of release, an exploration of trust, or a space to act out fantasies of submission, vulnerability, and control. In Femdom, the Queen is the dominant and the man is the submissive, so it is the exploration of the interaction or power exchange between the dominant and the submissive. BDSM actions occur in sessions called "play," "scene," or "session." During this time, you and your Queen will engage in practices such as inflicting pain or humiliation or being restrained. You can experiment with practice which involves physical sensations or just verbal.

In order to explore BDSM and Femdom, you and your Queen must be open and willing to explore their psychological connection. BDSM is both a physical and emotional experience, and for submissives in Femdom, it's about giving your Queen the power to empower you. Submission is a choice, a choice to let go of who you are and become who the other believes you should be. But surrendering can be more difficult than we think, which is why it is the Queen's role to free you, the submissive, from the constraints of your own mind. And with great power comes great responsibility.

The Queen, as the dominant, is not merely a sadist who inflicts pain for their own pleasure. She is a caregiver and helps you to open up, relax, and feel safe to explore your masochistic desires. Of course, fear is all part of the exchange, but you must first surrender to the idea of fear before you can truly explore it.

Additionally, BDSM is about pushing your limits—not passing them. You explore your limits with your Queen in all forms of sexual activity, comfort, consent, and pleasure. While you explore, think about each of your goals in this BDSM relationship. Are you both aware of each other's boundaries and intentions? Have you communicated your needs before and afterplay or scenes? The most crucial point is that all activities are done with consent.

Femdom allows FLR couples to explore each other's needs, desires, and limits. You can push the intensity in your sex lives safely without fear of detrimental results. Because you and your Queen are exploring spanking, restraints, CBT, anal play, pet play, fetishes and more in the safety of your relationship, Femdom is instrumental in helping you both reach a new level of intimacy and trust. The focus is turned inward as your Queen is focused on you and you are controlled by her.

No type of power play is considered "abnormal" so long as you are both willing participants and it doesn't interfere with other aspects of life. You can make the experience whatever you want. A little power playing with BDSM can be just what the doctor ordered for a stagnating sexual relationship. It can shift the dynamic, create a healthy sense of sexual drama, and improve emotional intimacy.

The fundamental principles for BDSM require informed consent. Since the 1980s, many practitioners and organizations have adopted the motto "safe, sane and consensual," commonly abbreviated SSC, which means that everything is based on safe activities. That all participants are of sufficiently sound mind to consent, and that all participants do consent. It is mutual consent that makes a clear legal and ethical distinction between BDSM and such crimes as sexual assault.

Another code is Risk Aware Consensual Kink (RACK). This emphasizes that each individual is responsible for his or her own well-being. In general, BDSM play is usually structured such that it is possible for the consenting partner to withdraw his or her consent at any point during a scene with the use of the safe word. Negotiations will take place before the scene, so that you and your Queen establish the ground rules for the activity. There is also aftercare where you talk about the experience they had in the scene. Since I believe that communication is critical in any relationship, discussing how the experience is important will provide more opportunity for intimacy and bonding.

BDSM has emerged from the underground and is now out in the open. It involves a power exchange and has the potential to make relationships more sexually fulfilling, but just like all relationships, it's a matter of communicating wants and desires. People are not just talking about it more openly than they did in the past, but they are also practicing BDSM in their sex lives. Studies reveal 58 percent of users have a desire to participate in BDSM. In addition, people who engage in BDSM neither have more pathological personality traits nor insecure attachment styles. Neither are most of them experiencing negative feelings nor being driven by harmful motivations in their engagement of intense sensation play.

BDSM also involves discipline in which the goal is to teach you, the sub, to learn discipline, self-restraint, and servitude. You will deepen your understanding of how to worship the Queen, and she will also learn how to ignite your desire to submit and to experience her dominance. In BDSM, there are two things that must not be confused — the disciplining of the sub and sadomasochism (S&M), which involves giving pain or torture to a "sub" for sexual enjoyment. Punishments for disciplining are in response to violations of predetermined rules or for otherwise displeasing your Queen. Punishment is considered necessary, as without it, you may repeat mistakes and thus not improve in your role as submissive.

S&M, or sadomasochism, is more about the sub's desire for pain as part of the sexual arousal he receives. So, you and your Queen will negotiate the type of BDSM activities you will want to participate in. The reason the two branches of BDSM work so well in Femdom is because part of female led life involves you learning how to serve the Queen and her desires. And the second part is the sexual arousal you experience from things she may do to assert her power over you. Learning how to better serve your Queen may utilize discipline if it's something you both agree to. Fully submitting to your Queen is where you will witness a transformative experience.

What Is Subspace?

The subspace is the state of mind achieved by you, the submissive, during intense play. It is similar to an orgasm, and everyone will have their own experience. However, it is common to experience feelings of euphoria, almost like a high or drunk feeling, and reality fades away as the mind relaxes, and the only thing you're focused on is your Queen.

This state of mind can often be compared to a meditative state in which your breathing becomes shallow, and you feel deeply relaxed. So much so that pain thresholds often become higher or non-existent, and you may feel as though you are having an out-of-body experience.

It is in this state that you can begin to push your limits to reach new heights, but your Queen must remain in control and be aware of when you have reached your limits. If it's going past your limit, it is important to use your safe word, as you may be in such a trance that you are unable to specify how you are feeling. Once you say your safe word, all activity must stop. Femdom play with safety is important so that you have an enjoyable experience with subspace.

Common Terms in BDSM:

Aftercare: Aftercare is post-play activities in which you and your Queen will check in on one another to ensure the scene was enjoyable, tend to any issues, hesitations, and emotional needs, and communicate on how it all went.

BDSM: Stands for Bondage, Discipline, Sadism, and Masochism, and is an umbrella term for any kinky play that involves a consensual power exchange. In Femdom, it is the branch of BDSM where the Queen takes the dominant role while the man is the submissive.

Bondage: Bondage is when you, the submissive, is tied up by your Queen who is a dominant partner. Bondage is frequently part of impact play, because tying up the submissive, who then consensually cannot move, adds to the thrill of the scene.

Dom Drop and Sub Drop: During a BDSM scene, endorphins and adrenaline run high for all partners. As a result, like a crash from a drug, the submissive and dominant partner may experience a comedown immediately after or even a few days later. All parties involved have a responsibility to tend to their partner during their drop.

D/S: Refers to dominance and submission. Your Queen takes on the dominant, or top role. In impact play, this is the person inflicting the spanks or other forms of play. You are the submissive, or the person receiving the impact on their body.

Edge play: Edge play refers to BDSM activities that push the limit of what is considered safe, sane, and consensual. This often refers to activities involving bodily fluids and blood. Pushing things to the edge. Care must be taken when indulging in this.

Hard Limits: Your hard limits are activities that are absolutely off-limits and should be communicated to your partner prior to play.

Kink: A kink refers to any sexual interest that is outside the heterosexual vanilla norm.

Play: Play is a word used within the kink community to refer to any erotic activity, from penetrative intercourse to impact play.

RACK: Stands for Risk Aware Consensual Kink and is the guideline all kinky play should follow. It means all parties consent and understand the risks they are taking.

Safe word: A safe word is a term agreed upon by you and your Queen that indicates it's time to immediately stop the play. A safe word is used instead of "stop" or "no." They should be unique like "pineapple" or "turquoise" so they can be easily recognized and not slurred during moaning or orgasm. The safe word can be anything your Queen and you decide for your own use, but you must communicate it so there is an agreement to stop.

SCC: Stands for Safe, Sane, and Consensual. It is another acronym for safety guidelines, although RACK is more commonly used today because what is considered safe and sane varies from person to person.

Scene: A scene refers to the time when the agreed kinky game takes place.

Soft Limits: Soft limits are things you are curious about but hesitant to try. Perhaps in the future you'll want to try them, but as of now, it's a no. Your limits may change with time.

BDSM works with Femdom because it provides a framework for you and the Queen to explore types of power play including discipline, domination and submission, humiliation, pet play, edge play, fetishes, and more. Consent from you and your Queen must be agreed on before exploring BDSM.

CHAPTER 5
History of BDSM and Femdom

BDSM and Femdom seem to have begun in Mesopotamia, where the Goddess of Fertility, Inanna, whipped her human subjects and caused them to do a frenzy dance. This painful whipping caused intercourse and led to pleasure amidst the dance and the moans. The ancient Romans also believed in flogging, and they had a Tomb of Flogging where women flogged each other to celebrate Bacchus or Dionysus, the God of Wine & Fertility.

The ancient scriptures of the Kama Sutra also explain the practice of biting, slapping, gnawing, etc. Furthermore, throughout the Middle Ages, flagellation was popular and based on the idea of extreme love and passion. It was also believed to help people get rid of evil and sins.

The history of BDSM dates back to 490 BC. In Italy, the Whipping Tomb paintings were discovered and showed a scene of two men getting pleasure while sexually flogging a woman. The scene is reminiscent of Dionysus as the god of the grape-harvest, winemaking and wine, and of fertility in Greek mythology. He is considered "the liberator," and his wine, music, and ecstatic dance free his followers from self-conscious fear and concern and subvert the oppressive restraints of the powerful. Those who partake in his mysteries are believed to become possessed and empowered by the god himself.

The Etruscan burial site was called the Tomba della Fustigazione or "Tomb of Flogging" after its depictions of eroticized flagellation. These may have been related to the pre-Roman holiday of Lupercalia, the original pagan Valentine's Day, which features light public spankings and whippings instead of, or in addition to, the traditional kisses and candy of our modern Valentine's Day. In Medieval times, with overt pagan pleasures denied, Catholic saints and penitents indulged in auto-flagellation to reach states of mystical consciousness that bordered on the erotic.

And it's not just Italians. For thousands of years, Taoist Chinese have engaged in a similar ritual of spanking and whipping during the Spring Festivals of their Lunar New Year, the stated purpose of which is to get rid of "bad luck." The Indian Kama Sutra contains multiple descriptions of how to "strike" your partner's buttocks, as well as other body parts, during sex. Tibetan monks have long whipped each other for medicinal and spiritual purposes. In Latvia, Sweden, Hungary, Slovakia, Poland, and Czech Republic, it is customary for the young men to awaken the young ladies on Palm Sunday, Good Friday, Shrove Tuesday, or Easter Monday by dousing them with water and spanking them on the butt and legs with colorful Easter whips in a playfully aggressive way.

Later on, Sadism is named after Marquis de Sade (1740-1814), a French nobleman and soldier, who spent many years in prisons and asylums, much of it for sexual behavior that was considered abhorrent. He also wrote novels describing scenes of sexual cruelty. Next was Freud, and though he is not considered the authority on sex and sexuality, it would be foolish to deny the impact he had on society. Although Freud's theories and therapy were rooted in misogyny and opinion, he did something no other psychological professional in the Western world had done before him: He openly talked about sex and sexual identity development. This laid the groundwork for our current sexual world and profession, one in which we can now talk about sex and have space to assist clients working through sexuality-related concerns.

Elizabeth Ehrmann wrote of Freud's three forms of masochism in her study titled, "The Economic Problem of Masochism." In this study, Freud distinguished three forms of masochism: erotogenic, feminine, and moral. Freud regarded the first two forms of masochism as secondary to sadism, and a turning inward of this upon the self because you enjoy having pain inflicted upon yourself. The third kind, moral masochism, is different because it is not obviously erotic, not physical, and has no special relations to significant persons. According to Freud, it is the suffering or self-injury itself that matters, no matter who inflicts it, whether it is a person or fate.

The moral form of masochism plays an extensive part in social life because it is an abusive internal monologue, and in analysis, it represents perhaps the most difficult problem to solve. Freud proposed the concept of "moral masochism," in which the practice was recast as the unconscious desire for punishment borne of guilt. So, from here, it was not related to sexuality but in a category all on its own. Ehermann has also written in the article "Sadomasochism According to Freud's Psychosexual Stages of Development Theory" that according to Freud, the combination of children being sexual, and perhaps the repeated act of spanking, whipping, or beating, is believed to lead to a life of sadomasochism.

If Freud's theory is correct, children who have experienced spankings or whippings will tend to be or would desire to be a sadomasochist, hence an interest in pain and spanking in adulthood. There is no doubt that spanking wakes up something inside us, particularly those who are very aroused and excited by it.

Through Freud's psychosexual stages of development theory, a better understanding of the sexual deviation, "sadomasochism" will ideally be reached. The six psychosexual stages of development are oral, anal, phallic, latent, and genital. Through each of these different stages, Freud believed that sexual outcomes originate. In addition, Freud's Oedipus complex offers some clues to the desire for spanking. The Oedipus complex explains the emotions and ideas that the mind keeps in the unconscious, via dynamic repression, that concentrates upon a child's desire to have sexual relations with the parent of the opposite sex for example, males attracted to their mothers, and females attracted to their fathers.

The Oedipus complex also suggests that boys will be fearful of their fathers, and this is resolved through identification where they copy their fathers' behavior. The same occurs with the girl and their mothers. Therefore, it is this identification which leads to boys and girls — of parents who are aggressive and administer punishment, like spanking — to also have a similar desire and exhibit similar behavior. If a boy grew up with his father being dominated by a strong mother, then he will crave this role in his own partner. Today, many men and women are raised in single-parent households where the mother takes control and must be the strong dominant parent. This explains why there is an increased number of men craving Female Led Relationships and more women desiring to lead the relationship. It also explains the desire of men to be dominated in bed by their women.

The psychologist Roy Baumeister noted that the nonsexual behaviors often characterized as "masochistic" differ qualitatively from sexual masochism in that it tends to be self-destructive and self-defeating. Sexual masochism, on the other hand, is neither destructive nor self-defeating. Sexual masochists neither seek nor regularly experience injury. Rather, they engage in carefully negotiated rituals of humiliation and the infliction of pain through spanking and discipline. Data suggest that sexual masochists as a group are generally normal in all other aspects of their lives and psychologically healthy.

In a recent survey of over 1,500 adults, more than one-third of women and more than one-quarter of men reported having fantasized about being spanked or whipped. There are many additional theories for masochism, which includes any behavior that runs counter to our daily habits will be considered arousing. In other words, if you spend your days being powerful and in control, the feeling of powerlessness and the loss of control will be arousing.

In terms of torture, Stanley Milgram was one of the first people to study it in the Milgram experiment on obedience to authority figures, a series of social psychology experiments conducted by Yale University. The study measured the willingness of men to respond to an authority figure to conduct acts on others against their conscience. The results indicated that a high proportion of men were willing to do this. It suggests that under the right circumstances, and with the appropriate encouragement and setting, men will respond to an authority figure and be completely obedient — as in the case of the woman who is their Queen.

Based on these theories, and the fact that the US divorce rate is at 60 percent, 83 percent of single-parent households are headed by the mother. Currently, one in four kids under 18 are raised without a father, or about 16.4 million children. So, a significant number of people are raised in single-parent homes where the mother is dominant. According to Freud's theory, men will have the desire for their mothers who generally now have to be strong independent women and will primarily do the disciplining, hence the man's desire for discipline from a strong woman in a Female Led Relationship.

In Freud's theory of identification, women will want to be like their mothers, hence they will naturally take charge and be assertive in their intent to do the disciplining. Merge these two and you get a very strong sexual desire for men to seek out strong women in a Female Led Relationship and their desire to engage in aggression, like being spanked by a partner capable of doing the spanking. It is my belief that there will be a growing trend for erotic spanking.

Research shows that men are responsible for over 90 percent of serious violent crimes, such as assaults, homicides, and violent robberies. Why is there such a large gender gap and is it likely to persist? One might imagine that lower violent crime rates for women reflects a generally lower level of aggression. Yet marriage researchers observe the opposite pattern. Women are more likely to pick fights with their husbands, are quicker to escalate verbal aggression, and are likely to use physical aggression than men.

Modern women are behaving much more like men when it comes to risk-taking and aggression. One sign of this phenomenon is greater involvement in contact sports and dangerous competitions, such as horse racing or car racing. According to Anthropologist Elizabeth Cashdan, societies where women compete more amongst each other, whether in occupations, or over spouses, their levels of stress hormones and testosterone increase. These women enjoy taking charge, and they admit to having no problem being aggressive with men.

In the 17th century, two German authors made their name in spanking research: the German physician Johann Heinrich Meibom, who wrote a best-selling treatise on the use of flogging as a medical and sexual stimulant, and German medical botanist and poet Kristian Frantz Paullini, whose *Flagellum Salutis* praised flagellation for its curative use in treating diseases as diverse as melancholia, paralysis, toothache, sleepwalking, deafness, and nymphomania, as well as for pleasure and sexual arousal.

From the 18th century onward there have been many establishments for dominatrices and Femdom throughout the United Kingdom. One of the most famous dominatrix during the early 19th century was Mrs. Teresa Berkley. Her clients were wealthy men and women in London, and she is famous for inventing the Berkley horse.

In the 60s, Ms. Monique Von Cleef known as the Queen of Humiliation operated "The House of Pain" where many men from all walks of life visited her in search of her BDSM services. Since then, there are hundreds of thousands of dominatrices worldwide.

What began as secret businesses has now exploded into the mainstream in movies, TV, YouTube, and Netflix.

CHAPTER 6
Why Men Crave Femdom

Why do men crave Femdom? Men have been fascinated by Femdom and the power of a strong woman for decades. The dominatrix, either in person or online, is how most men get their first experience during their teenage years or early adulthood. I believe that a man's true nature is his deepest desire to submit to a powerful Queen. He will fight it, ignore it, hate it because of patriarchal conditioning, but once he recognizes that female dominance is what he craves, he embraces it and is set free. He is able to express his innermost fantasies, and we see this more in social media postings as well as in their choices of porn.

Why is Femdom porn exploding at almost one million searches a month if it were not for the increased desire for Femdom and female domination? Men's true desires are expressed in their fantasies, and they explore these fantasies through the consumption of porn when there is an absence of a strong dominant woman in their lives. A man learns early on that complete submission to a Queen is what he desires most in life and because he is constantly searching for his life purpose. Femdom aligns with his deepest desires to surrender to a powerful Queen.

From the dawn of time, men went out into the wild, faced grave danger, hunted, and provided for his family. Why? Because he knows that through this daily act he serves and protects his Queen. Men were expected to go to war and fight in armies, which he did to fulfill his duty to protect the Queen. If men did not have this inner desire to serve and protect women, women would have been trained a long time ago to do the same.

For men, the Femdom experience is their greatest fantasies come to life. A man's desire to be dominated by a great woman is so strong he willingly begins his exploration by submitting to a dominatrix. He will explore pain, submit to her whims, and even pay to feel the fear and excitement of being dominated. The thrill of the unknown and the anticipation is all just too irresistible for him. Men's fantasies are expressions of their innermost desires, so each session with his Queen involving domination and submission triggers him and allows him to fully explore his deepest desires. When a man finally finds the Queen of his dreams, he can now move from intermittent triggers in domination and submission sessions to daily life. He now gets to live his true fantasies every single day.

What could be better than a relationship with the dominant Queen of his dreams and an opportunity to explore female led life each day? I believe that it is unhealthy for men to suppress these urges and never have an opportunity to experience their desire to submit to a Queen because of patriarchal conditioning or a belief that Femdom is taboo. It's important to understand the submissive male to understand how the female domination lifestyle is fulfilling to him.

Not every female domination relationship is the same. Some are more advanced than others based on the desires of the individuals involved. Some couples keep it confined to the bedroom, and female domination is a way to spice up their sex lives. Others take it outside the bedroom and into their everyday life. To these couples, female domination is more of a lifestyle and a belief system. Regardless of the degree of the female domination activities, I have found that a majority of the couples who practice female domination claim to have better marriages and relationships than they did before getting involved. They claim to enjoy deeper intimacy and more fulfilling sex lives.

Some men also desire in Femdom punishment, such as spanking and whipping, forced feminization, dressing in women's clothing, and being treated like a weak, pathetic sissy, humiliation, pegging, water sports like forced enemas or golden showers, chastity (e.g., wearing the chastity cage), confinement (e.g., being locked in a cage), and more. The range of domination will vary from couple to couple, so it's integral to be very clear, what level of Femdom you desire and communicate with your Queen right from the start.

What is at the heart of it all is that men want to worship his woman by tending to her physical and sexual needs and they are willing to be made into a domesticated servant to their Queens. Above all, men long for a powerful, superior woman to whom they can completely surrender and devote their lives to service. I was extremely fascinated by the Netflix show *Inventing Anna*. Here is a woman, labeled a con woman, who could keep men entirely under her spell. How is 26-year-old

Annad, able to keep her boyfriend, a Silicon Valley startup tycoon, under spell, that he wishes to tend to her every need and take care of her to the tune of millions of dollars. She commands respect and demands to be treated like a Queen from the start. She doesn't just demand it from every person she meets — she expects it.

Men cannot resist an intelligent woman, who holds herself to the standard of Queen in all things. It isn't the money spent on a Queen that is the point, but rather that for centuries, powerful women have been able to control powerful men and bring them to their knees in acts of complete submission and surrender. We think of Cleopatra, Anne Boleyn, Queen Elizabeth I, Catherine the Great, and so many more. Men, no matter your status, education, alpha or beta or upbringing, you will desire the experience of a powerful Queen, and now you can have it daily.

CHAPTER 7
Why Women Like Femdom

Why do women like Femdom? Femdom places the Queen in the power position and gives a woman the unique opportunity to benefit from her man's desire to be dominated. It's freedom to do what you will and have your every desire fulfilled. All women desire power. I believe it's the reason they pursue the power of beauty. Most women spend a lifetime chasing beauty but few experience the power in their own day-to-day interactions with men through their attitudes, personality, and intelligence.

A man is required to prove his devotion to his Queen, and one of the ways he can do this is by submitting to her leadership. When the Queen recognizes this submission, she is free to step into her power position as a true leader. A submissive man welcomes opportunities to show submission to the Queen. It is a myth that submission is a weakness. Rather it takes strength and willpower to put aside your own desires as a man to focus on hers. But by doing this, both alpha and beta men experience a transformation in their relationships or marriage by just making this change.

Life has meaning and purpose when you are responding to your true deep desire to serve a powerful woman. You help your Queen emerge as a leader through your willingness to serve her. Think of a general who can go in service to his Queen by leading an army. Do we view this as a weakness? Never. It's the ultimate act of courage and bravery. So, too, is the man who makes it his mission to make his Queen the happiest woman on the planet.

Women love Femdom because there is a power exchange, and the Queen is in charge in a Female Led Relationship. She has the power and the opportunity to exert her power on her man, especially during sex. He has the goal of fully satisfying her needs. This can be a great turn on for both men and women. Also, let's face it, dominance is sexy. Domination during sex intensifies sexual drive, and powerful women drive men crazy. A woman in a position of power is the desire of every man, particularly to the man who has dedicated his life to service his Queen.

According to a new paper published in the journal *Social Psychological and Personality Science* by Joris Lammers and Roland Imhoff, social power reduces inhibition, and this goes for both men and women allowing them to crave alternative lifestyles and fantasies. Since women are experiencing much more power in society, they are enjoying Femdom and the feeling of being in the power position in their relationships. Researchers Lammers and Imhoff point out that while many people have sadomasochistic impulses, they don't act on them, as those impulses go against social norms. Traditional gender roles say that men are primarily active and women passive. In fantasies, men are more likely to crave submission, and women will crave domination. Power frees people from their inhibitions, and thereby increases sadomasochistic thoughts in men and women. Powerful women will explore this through Femdom.

There is also a spiritual dimension to Female Domination. Females have a power over males and that power is not physical. That power is expressed through sexually, but it resides in the mind and originates in the spirit. This power is within, and women need to release it. I believe that when both men and women step into their rightful roles, Queens as dominant and men as submissive and supportive gentlemen are able to explore their higher energies and the interaction becomes spiritual.

During dating, men shower their Queen with flowers and gifts. A man will romance the woman and write her poetry and sing her songs. Even macho and overly masculine men will show their softer side around a Queen whom they really want to conquer and be in a long-term relationship with. In dating, a man will rise to new heights to impress her, indulge her, and will agree to do whatever she wants to do, just to be near her.

But once they become married, this often changes. He takes her for granted, stops showering her with gifts, and becomes selfish. He often goes out with friends, plays video games all day, ignoring the woman who is supposed to be the most important person in his life. Arguments and disagreements increase, and sex, which used to be exhilarating, becomes boring. Once the man gets his sexual release, it's time to go to sleep. Forget about her.

What happened to the passion? Often in normal relationships, women don't realize that the reason she has him under a spell with her beauty and her sexuality is because she is the dominant one during dating. Women naturally have the power during dating as her sexual energy caused the man to become submissive toward her.

However, in normal relationships, married or in a serious relationship, women tend to take on the submissive role and allow men to be the dominant because of societal conditioning. Once this happens, everything changes, and I believe this is the beginning of the problem. She begins to feel ignored, overwhelmed and sexually unsatisfied and this begins a vicious cycle which eventually leads to more and more unhappiness. Men begin to take the woman for granted because what he wanted all along was a Queen. The opposite happens in a Female Led Relationship. Men have already chosen to be submissive, so they have already agreed to their Queen having free reign over them. Femdom just takes this to a whole new level. During sex, heightened levels of sexual pleasure begin once the woman assumes this role of dominance and adds in many thrilling sexual Femdom activities. It is important for the Queen to assert authority as leader during sex as this portrays to you that she knows what she wants and is going to have it. This will make you eager to please and submit. It adds an element of adventure and fear, which can be extremely arousing.

Queens need to feel empowered and excited to take charge. You can encourage this by showing service to your Queen in daily gestures like supporting her and expressing how much you desire to feel her power. Keep the sexy alive, no matter what. I instruct couples all the time to ensure they are having sex and being sexy multiple times a week. Each day is a new day to do something sexy for your Queen and encourage her to step into her power. Compliment her, surprise her, listen to her, be of service, be understanding, be empathetic and make her feel like she is the most special person in the world.

It is normal for sex in long-term relationships to get monotonous and repetitive, so Femdom shakes things up and allows the Queen to have the control, which is her deepest desire. I feel that Femdom appeals to the core nature of a female led woman, which is to have complete power over her man. Just as children get tired of their old toys, adults also get bored and tired of carrying out the same, repetitive sexual routine and styles without the introduction of something new or adventurous.

Femdom can make things very intimate since the Queen is in total control and the man is vulnerable. It brings about freshly ignited feelings that come with trying different things. This creates intimacy and transports you both to a whole new world of sexual intimacy and bonding in ways you never expected. Many men have testified to feeling satisfied and fulfilled when they are dominated by their Queen. A certain stimulus is ignited when a man is physically and mentally controlled because this triggers the dopamine receptors into action, bringing about sexual pleasure, which is an exciting time. When your Queen sees that you are enthusiastic and excited about your submissive role, she feels empowered to step into her role as your Queen and superior leader. You change the dynamic when you decide to show your devotion to her and acknowledge her as your supreme leader and ruler in your relationship or marriage. She feels inspired to become someone you will adore and respect daily.

CHAPTER 8
Domination and Submission

W hat does domination and submission mean in a relationship? What are the benefits, roles, and rules of this type of relationship? When it comes to defining and understanding domination and submission, people, especially those in vanilla relationships, often think of the movie *Fifty Shades of Grey*. The relationship between the two main characters revolves around power dynamic, power play, and bondage and discipline. Christian Grey is a male dominant partner, whereas Anastasia Steele plays a submissive role.

However, if you analyze what happens in the movie, you will see that Anastasia's power grows throughout the series and in the end, she appears to be the one in control. She even puts an end to him being allowed to spank her, which showed her taking charge and making the rules.

This example is much more consistent with domination and Femdom. Similarly, today the tables are turning with more women assuming the dominant position in relationships, households, and in the workplace. In a Female Led Relationship, this can be anywhere from her being a

Queen and you her submissive gentleman, to her being a full dominatrix and you being a slave.

Many people new to domination and submission wonder if this kind of relationship exists in real life or if it's just limited to the bedroom. How does it work? As I have indicated in several of my previous books, Female Led Relationships are growing, and hundreds of thousands of couples worldwide are exploring.

The dominant Queen is the leader. She calls the shots. She guides and leads you in all aspects of life and the relationship. You, the man, is the submissive and you take your guidance from her. Your role is to serve. Men who do not understand this dynamic are stuck in a patriarchal world, and they may think that submission means succumbing to abuse from women. This could not be further from the truth. Couples in a Female Led Relationship have reported more happiness and a deeper connection with more sexual intimacy than they ever thought possible. They are happier and more fulfilled in a relationship based on domination and submission.

In the D/S relationship, there are strict rules that both people follow but they need not be extreme. It's important that rules are respected and followed. What we don't realize is that domination and submission are natural. In almost every relationship, there is one partner who is more submissive and the other who is more dominant. Couples who identify as being into a D/S relationship tend to include power play in their sex life. They will often explore aspects of BDSM and different types of play, which is what makes these relationships exciting. You can explore all areas of domination and submission, which provides more ways to increase the excitement and adventure in long-term relationships and marriages.

Let's face it, boredom and monotony are real challenges that couples must overcome. By being open to exploring different types of dominant and submissive interactions, you can minimize the boredom by adding so many new ideas to spice up your sex life and daily life. Each day represents a new opportunity for couples to explore this power dynamic and add different types of play into their sex life. One night is for spanking, another is for an "eyes wide shut" party, another is for bondage, another could be kink night, etc.

How much does one's life change in a regular vanilla relationship? Quite often couples get stuck in a rut of daily life and work routines. Household responsibilities and kids make it even more challenging. But when you decide to engage in submission and make it your life purpose, you have an added goal to aspire to. You have new things that challenge you at home. One of the reasons why people become workaholics and addicted to work is because they lack challenge and excitement in daily home life. But when exploring domination and submission, you and your Queen have real goals and interests outside of work, which brings the two of you closer together.

Domination and submission can help improve communication because you are engaging in discussions about your fantasies, likes, and dislikes. You are constantly exploring new ways to increase the excitement. Perhaps being dominant is new to your Queen. She's just beginning to experience what it's like to take the lead, give out orders, and control the relationship. Maybe you will still need to work on learning how to submit, worship, and obey her. Constantly engaging in discussion about these experiences offers more opportunity to communicate, particularly about sexy things. How many times a week are you spending, discussing what turns you on, your fantasies, and exploring new ways of changing things up? Now you can.

For most people, being dominant or submissive will be something that they only do occasionally, for example, just in pre-arranged scenes — often, but not always, involving sex. Such scenes could involve any kind of exchange of power. For example, you, the submissive person, might serve food to your Queen or give her a massage. Your Queen may decide to give you orders, restrain you, or administer punishment if you've been a bad boy. There are lots of power-based role-playing, such as teacher and student, cop and robber, or pirate and captive. Some couples decide to indulge in D/S only during sex or for a weekend, but for many couples in Femdom or Female Led Relationships, domination and submission is a lifestyle and will occur daily.

Domination and submission in relationships can occur within a framework of elaborate rules of conduct. such as you, the submissive man, will come home, get changed into your Queen's preferred attire, present yourself for inspection when she returns, prepare the house, kids, and dinner for her return and ensure all daily chores are completed to her satisfaction. D/S rules can continue to the bedroom where you will service your Queen with oral pleasure first until she is fully satisfied or until she decides you can enter her and orgasm.

Your Queen will make all decisions about family outings and activities, chores, division of responsibilities, and she may control the finances. You may both decide there should be specific repercussions for transgressions like spanking for punishment or other forms of behavior modification. When it comes to practices and activities to explore domination and submission, there are countless ideas you can implement into your relationship — as long as everything is done with consent from both you and the Queen.

CHAPTER 9
What Does It Mean to Be Submissive?

What does it mean to be submissive? There is a beautiful surrender that comes when a man allows himself to be vulnerable and submissive to his Queen. When men experience negative life occurrences, it can harden them and cause them to go inward and bottle up frustrations inside of them. However, Femdom can help them to relax their rigid boundaries because their Queen essentially takes control. They have someone they can trust to take the lead, which takes the pressure off them.

A man's true nature is to submit to a dominant woman, and he desires to find someone so powerful that he has no choice but to make it his life purpose to serve her. It is only through this service that men can fully become aware of their true nature and learn more about their inner desires. The reason men begin to explore Femdom early through porn is they have this inner motivation but don't quite understand why. They often begin their exploration as teenagers, then continue into adulthood. I also believe it explains the increased interest in milfs, sex with older women, and the desire to experience being dominated.

Today, hundreds of thousands of men are embracing a female led lifestyle. Why? Because they find joy in being a submissive man to a strong woman. The assumption is that submissive men give up all responsibility for themselves. There is a misconception that they become doormats who cannot stand up for themselves and are taken advantage of by predatory dominant Queens. This is absolutely false. Submissive men are extremely strong, capable men who simply want to submit to the most important woman in their lives. Many of them crave submission as a way to temporarily escape the huge responsibilities they take on in their normal lives. This is why more couples are exploring this dynamic of domination and submission within BDSM and Femdom.

The subspace is important for submissives. In BDSM, subspace refers to a specific kind of space with its own rules, texture, and properties—a kind of altered reality which usually takes place in the mind, although changes in the surrounding physical space can make a difference as well. This is why, for instance, people go out of their way to set up private playrooms and dungeons. These settings make it easier to get into the mood of an interaction—to enter a psychological state where all the worries, cares, underlying thoughts, and emotions are stripped away, and your deepest, darkest fantasies can become reality.

The subspace is the specific psychological state of mind that the submissive partner enters into during a scene with a dominant partner. To enter this subspace, the submissive must be completely comfortable with your Queen as the dominant and completely give up control to her. In many ways, getting into a subspace follows many of the same steps of practicing basic mindfulness; you must be 100 percent present with your Queen and in the moment.

Subspace is that feeling of utter presence when all of your senses are heightened, and your mind and emotions are totally wrapped up in the suspense of the moment. For submissive men, entering subspace is an experience that melts away all of your worries and fears. You don't have to think about anything or make tough decisions. You just need to obey your Queen and go with the flow. Most submissive men agree that they feel a sense of euphoria, a warm, ecstatic glow. In a true Femdom session, men experience the afterglow, which can last for hours, even weeks. It creates feelings of love, attachment, belonging, and well-being. You and your dominant Queen will share a special connection.

Psychologically, this sort of play is very healing too. Submissive men usually carry sexual desires that they feel they must hide away. But this allows them a free space to explore those fantasies without fear of judgment. A loving female authority who is in charge works for submissive men, and they find them tremendously sexy and attractive.

There is so much to the psychology of Femdom. When it comes to surrendering, there is so much to the psychology of Femdom. Much of the pleasure and arousal is generated in our erotic desires, fantasies, and memories. When Femdom involves role-play with dominance and submission, you and your Queen explore the dynamic of power and surrender. The trust between the submissive man and his Queen is so incredible that when he gives himself up to her entirely, it is almost like an out-of-body experience. Reality melts away and nothing matters but her next move and command. This can only be experienced through true submission and learning to be submissive transforms your relationship or marriage in ways you never thought possible.

When you are new to BDSM and Femdom, you will experience some obstacles that often stem from patriarchal conditioning and an inability to submit completely. Some of these negative behaviors are discussed below.

Topping from the Bottom

Topping from the bottom refers to when you, the submissive, are trying to take control of the scene and not truly submitting to your Queen. When you are new to Femdom or BDSM, there will be a tendency for you to want to act out and try to control the dynamic between you and your Queen.

Topping from the bottom means you are trying to give direction to or making decisions for the dominant in a way that goes against the predetermined power dynamic. You may not fully understand your role as submissive and it's important that you make it clear in your mind through your decision to submit to your Queen.

Topping from the bottom can destroy the connection and trust because your Queen cannot feel empowered and confident about her role as the dominant if she is constantly being questioned or judged. Here are some ways you can identify where you may be topping from the bottom include:

Contradicting your Queen. You are constantly questioning or trying to change your Queen's mind about the decision they have made, without a valid reason. You are questioning her decisions daily and during sex or sessions.

Ignoring Your Queen. You purposely ignore your Queen or pretend you didn't hear the request and resume doing what you want to do is not appropriate. She requires that you acknowledge the request as soon as possible and follow out the command as best you can. You can always go back to what you were doing afterward. Your Queen is expecting your service at all times, not just when you want to give it.

You Only Do Something If You Benefit. Submission isn't about you expecting to get benefits or pleasing you directly. Doing things for her should be your pleasure and your goal is to do them correctly as requested. Conditional submission is topping from the bottom when you only choose to submit when it suits you. This behavior will eventually harm the relationship, so it is important to fully commit to submission right from the start.

You Decline Requests and Say No. As a submissive, it is fine for you to decline a request and say no if you are uncomfortable, but if your Queen gives you a reasonable request and it is within your negotiated terms to do so, then you shouldn't say no just because you don't feel like completing her request. A close addition to this is yelling, screaming or showing any kind of disrespectful behavior toward your Queen when she gives you an order or makes a request. This would also be topping from the bottom. It is perfectly fine for you to make requests in a respectful manner.

You and your Queen must have already specified how a session should proceed or discussed the rules in your Femdom relationship beforehand. If you, the submissive, are trying to control the relationship, you need to re-communicate those details and determine if further discussion is needed or if you're both in agreement. Topping from the bottom is a type of manipulation that isn't healthy for the relationship just as manipulation isn't healthy for any romantic or sexual relationship. It's not open or honest, and it doesn't help either person grow.

How to Deal with Topping from the Bottom

The first step is to recognize you're doing it, then have a conversation with your Queen about why it's hard to let go. Perhaps you need her encouragement and guidance to help you to feel more relaxed and reassured. Next, identify the areas where you're unable to let go of control and add that to your negotiations, which will happen during preparation for your session.

Your Queen will need to ensure adequate training is given and encourage positive behaviors and discourage the undesirable actions. You have every right to express your needs to your Queen. Letting her know you need help or space is allowed. Asking for more kink or less of it is also okay.

Remember, your Queen also has to consent to it, but you should always have the freedom to share what you need and want in the moment and in the relationship. "Renegotiations" are simply having conversations with your Queen. These conversations are normal parts of a growing, healthy relationship. As a submissive, you're allowed to request a change. Your Dominant must consent to the change but wanting it doesn't make you less submissive.

In the beginning of your D/S relationship, you and your Dominant set up the rules, protocols, and punishments. Some of this was based on previous experience or personal preference. No plan stays the same forever. What you thought you wanted or needed will likely change. Maybe you discovered that certain things have a negative impact on you. Hell, maybe you totally accept punishment as a concept but want to understand why it's happening now.

All of these and many other conversations about your rules, protocols, and punishments are your right to have. Your Femdom relationship isn't a dictatorship; it's a partnership between you and your Queen. To continue giving your consent, you can and should talk about every single part of your dynamic. Yes, even the rules and the punishments you don't love.

CHAPTER 10
What is Punishment in Femdom?

P unishment is a behavior modification tool used in domination and submission training. You, the submissive, must be disciplined when you've defied a boundary or disobeyed an order or crossed a boundary. In Female Led Relationships and Femdom, it is important for the Queen to lay out the specific rules and boundaries as well as the expected behavior.

Though couples will choose to engage in different things, each one is free to determine the type and severity of punishments they want to use — and the options are essentially endless. For example, if the submissive partner is a "brat" and he is a sub who purposely enjoys disobeying the Queen's rules, she may decide to use some appropriate punishment.

Punishment can include removal of privileges, spankings, slapping, choking, use of restraints, or forcing you into sexual acts with consent. You and your Queen decide what will be suitable. As with most deliciously kinky things, punishment is not just about pain, but also pleasure. Sexual punishment is when you know there is a part of you that is under-expressed, maybe from shame or fear. So, if you feel like you're being a naughty boy, being punished by your Queen allows you to live out that feeling, while also enjoying your naughty side.

Physical punishments provide a wide variety of punishment ideas. Why is this effective? You use punishment when the submissive does not obey and does not adhere to the specific expected behavior. The reason this is an issue is because the submissive needs to focus on what his Queen wants. Therefore, it is important for your Queen to provide punishment to ensure your behavior modification. When you yield and submit and accept your punishment, you will experience the power of female led life. You are submitting to your Queen's power to administer punishment.

One of the reasons you want to engage and accept punishment is because it is the only way you will be 100 percent devoted to your Queen. Your ability to accept the Queen's decisions and power to punish. You still need to consent to the punishment. Your Queen can only punish you if you consent, but once you give your consent, you must submit to her power. Punishment will help you to grow and it is a necessary part of your training. To engage in proper effective punishment, check out my book *Spanking* for you and your Queen so that both of you are aware of what is expected and the rules of engaging in effective punishment.

Some nonphysical punishments may include verbal degradation, humiliation, removal of privileges—you are not allowed to go out with the boys, watch your favorite shows, play video games, masturbate, or watch porn. Chastity for a week could be punishment as well as reciting affirmations.

My book *Turning Point* gives you lots of ideas on how to use affirmations in your training.

Other effective punishment ideas include writing out lines. When I was in school, a popular punishment was having to stay behind and write the lines: "I will not do X and Y again." A relevant example would be: "I will never disrespect my Queen in public again." Your Queen may order you to write these lines 10 or 200 times.

She may also add chores you don't usually do. For example, you have to scrub the garage or bathroom. You may have to complete additional chores as well as your normal daily chores. You may also have extended time in animal play, or additional time-out in a corner or locked in a cage. Maybe you must be a man table for your Queen and her friends. Couples find interesting and exciting ways to sometimes make punishment become *fun*ishment. However, punishment as part of a serious behavior modification training regime will always be more disciplined and serious. What direction you and your Queen decide to take punishment must be agreed to by both of you. Nothing is off the table. There are a variety of ways you can use punishment to increase the intensity of your Femdom experience.

Corporal Punishment

Corporal punishment is a form of physical punishment that involves the deliberate infliction of pain as retribution for an offense, or for the purpose of disciplining or reforming a wrongdoer, or to deter unacceptable attitudes or behaviors. The term usually refers to methodically striking the offender with an implement, whether in judicial, domestic, or educational settings.

Different parts of the anatomy may be targeted, such as the buttocks — whether clothed or bare — have often been targeted for punishment, particularly in Europe and the English-speaking world.

The advantage is that these fleshy body parts are robust and can be chastised accurately, without endangering any bodily functions, and they heal well and relatively quickly. In some cultures, punishment applied to the buttocks entails a degree of humiliation, which may or may not be intended as part of the punishment. Hitting the back of the thighs and calves is at least as painful, if not more so, but this can cause more damage in terms of scars and bruising. The upper back and the shoulders have historically been a target for whipping (e.g., in the UK with the cat-o'-nine-tails in the Royal Navy and in some pre-1948 judicial punishments), and today generally in the Middle East and the Islamic world. The soles of the feet are extremely sensitive and flogging them has sometimes been done in the Middle East.

Flagellation also falls under the umbrella of BDSM, and this is the act of spanking. It involves flogging, whipping, or lashing and is the act of beating the human body with special implements, such as whips, lashes, rods, switches, and the cat o' nine tails. Typically, flogging is imposed on an unwilling subject as a punishment; however, it can also be given to willingly, or performed on oneself, in religious or sadomasochistic contexts. Usually, it is the butt or back that is struck but for a moderated subform of flagellation, described as bastinado, the soles of a person's bare feet are used as a target for beating. In some circumstances, the word "flogging" is used loosely to include any sort of corporal punishment, including birching and caning.

The Flagellation, in a Christian context, refers to an episode in the Passion of Christ prior to Jesus's crucifixion. The practice of mortification of the flesh for religious purposes has been utilized by members of various Christian denominations since the time of the Great Schism in 1054. Nowadays, the instrument of penance is called a discipline, a cattail whip usually made of knotted cords, which is flung over the shoulders repeatedly during private prayer. In the 13th century, a group of Roman Catholics, known as the Flagellants, took self-mortification to extremes. These people would travel to towns and publicly beat and whip each other while preaching repentance. Since the nature of these demonstrations were quite morbid and disorderly, they were suppressed by the authorities. They continued to reemerge at different times up until the 16th century.

Flagellation was also practiced during the Black Plague as a means to purify oneself of sin and thus prevent contracting the disease. Pope Clement VI is known to have allowed the act for this purpose in 1348. Martin Luther, the Protestant Reformer, regularly practiced self-flagellation as a means of mortification of the flesh. So BDSM, flagellation, and spanking are all closely related.

CHAPTER 11
Femdom Activities

F emdom activities may draw on all areas of BDSM, ranging from D/S, humiliation, feminization, and different types of play, including impact play or spanking, animal play, pegging, foot worship, and more. Men are very turned on by erotic humiliation and the inadequacy of a small penis, so instead of feeling ashamed and angry about it, have fun with it with cuckolding and hotwifing, if it's what you and your Queen desire to explore.

Related activities include ballbusting, cock and ball torture (CBT), verbal degradation, forced chastity, and orgasm control. Light female domination scenarios may involve ageplay, funishment, and body worship, especially foot worship and anal play.

There are so many different areas to explore, and you and your Queen should discuss all aspects before engaging in any of it. The idea of adding Femdom to your Female Led Relationship is to begin to add more intense activities as part of your sex life and maybe even your daily life. Give each other time to indulge and experience your feelings about each part. You should already have some sort of FLR routine set before attempting to make things more intense.

Additional activities to spice up your sexual arousal may include forced facesitting or smothering, which tend to focus on you giving your Queen oral pleasure, or your Queen pegging you which is doing anal sex on you using a strap-on dildo. Even more intense than these are face-slapping, hair pulling, caning, heavy torture, dripping hot wax on the body and heavy whipping while you are saran wrapped. A step further from these would be spitting domination, or watersports like golden showers. As you move up in intensity, it is extremely important to ensure consent and to check in on how you both feel. There is no need to try everything in a short period of time but rather introduce new activities gradually.

One fairly common variation is rape fantasy for women where it's the warrior or fighter fantasy of the man. It's fight club in the bedroom. Your Queen wrestles or fights to show she is stronger. There are thousands of sites popping up now for mixed martial arts and females fighting men. This is particularly thrilling to a Queen who has a strong fitness routine, MMA (mixed martial arts) background, or great boxing skills. But again, be careful. Don't let things get out of control where you both end up in the hospital, and this is especially where your safe words come in handy. Everything you do should be controlled with established limits.

The idea is to use these added activities as ways to increase the intensity in your relationship but don't go overboard. Remember, you and your Queen are still in a loving Female Led Relationship with a desire to ignite the excitement and adventure. Each added activity represents a new step in your exploration together, and you must always discuss limits and boundaries. Especially in the beginning, it is important to respect any hesitations or concerns and always place each other's feelings at the top. Your relationship or marriage and your happiness is what's important. But what you choose to explore as a couple is your own prerogative as long as it's done safely.

CHAPTER 12
Erotic Humiliation

O ne area that is particularly interesting in Femdom is erotic humiliation, which is the consensual use of psychological humiliation in a sexual context. You would gain arousal or erotic excitement from the mixed and powerful emotions of being humiliated and demeaned by your Queen. She would gain a sense of power and happiness from shaming you. The humiliation need not be sexual in itself, as with many other sexual activities, rather, it is the feelings derived from it which are sought, regardless of the nature of the actual activity. It can be verbal or physical and can be relatively private or public.

There is a distinction between humiliation and dominance. The actual act of demeaning and humiliating must be present, not just domination. A person being humiliated is referred to as a bottom, and your Queen is often called the top since she is doing the humiliation. Other common names for bottom are slave or sub/submissive, and master/mistress for the top. Your Queen can determine what she wants to be called and she leads the activity. Humiliation comes into its own as a sexual force when the humiliation is desired over and above anything else.

If this is something you and your Queen are exploring, you will want much more of the experience of being humiliated more than the pain or discomfort of her dominating you. In spanking, when your Queen puts you over the knee, pulls down your pants, and immediately starts spanking you on your butt — that's the humiliation. A little different than in bed when you consent to be tied up and she whips you.

As such, humiliation encompasses a range of activities, including foot fetish or shoe fetish, body worship, spanking, and bondage. It can be as basic as the desire to kiss and massage feet as a precursor to sex, or it can be complex, involving role-play or public displays of subservience. I have had emails from readers who enjoy it when their wives and girlfriends have their men dressed only in aprons, clean their shoes, and kiss their feet.

The men may be required to wait in the corner of the room until they are called. There are so many variations that can be added to increase the excitement. It can also be for a set period of time or as an ongoing facet of a relationship. If you and your Queen prefer to engage in sexual humiliation, it can be divided into verbal and physical aspects.

Verbal aspects might include:

- Verbal belittlement, such as "slave," "boy," "girl," "missy," "pet."

- Insults and verbal abuse, such as "fat," "ugly," "stupid," "worthless."

- Degrading references such as "slut," "tart," "bitch," "faggot." and "whore."

- Criticizing body parts or behaviors, such as disparaging or cruel references to man boobs, facial appearance, genitalia or genital size, bottom, and criticizing mannerisms, such as how one walks, responses, or self-care standard.

- Having to ask permission for everyday activities such as using the toilet, eating, or spending money.

- Small penis humiliation, where scorn is addressed toward the supposed inadequacy of the male's genitals or his inability to please a woman (and by implication, his essential worthlessness as a man and his penis becomes an object of play).

- Forced repetition, such as being obliged to repeat back commands to confirm them. Repeating affirmations.

- Forced flattery, such as agreeing that every decision that the dominant makes is wise, correct, and justifiable while additionally praising the dominants physical and personality traits.

- Mockery and ridicule.

Physical Activities Might Include:

- Ejaculating, defecating, spitting, slapping or urinating on the bottom's body or face.

- Performance of menial tasks or abusive workload, such as cleaning the floors with a toothbrush.

- Requiring the frequent performance of passive/aggressive sexual services for the dominant, such as erotic massage, cunnilingus, analingus, or fellatio without expectations of reciprocal acts or intercourse.

- Detailed accountability and control or micro-managing as to time spent or activities done, including list of jobs to do, precise directions as to how the housework is to be performed, and exactly how to act and behave.

- Specific rituals to be adopted. This includes displays of subservience (e.g., lighting cigarettes, walking a pace behind your Queen), only speaking when spoken to, kneeling, or prostrating in front of the dominant when expecting orders, eating only after others have eaten, or eating on the floor, low status place to sleep, and a wide variety of body worship activities (e.g., kissing or licking your Queen's feet, boots, buttocks, anus, vulva, etc.) to express acknowledgment, subservience, shame, or even positive emotions, such as happiness or excitement.

- Suppressed freedom of movement. This may include never being able to leave the room in which the dominant is present without permission and may be forbidden to leave the house or "dungeon" in general for the duration of slavery or servitude.

- Detailed punishments for a variety of "infractions" or misbehavior, such as having to stand in a corner facing a wall for several hours, flogging or whipping, reduced rations, or forced exercise.

- Role-playing "lower status" beings such as animals, for example dogs, horses, donkeys, sheep, or babies.

- Spanking, whipping, restraint or other BDSM activities such as cock and ball torture (CBT).

- Restrictions on clothing—wearing just underwear, robe, suit or maids' uniform, feminizing, cross dressing, and/or sissification. You may be expected to be completely in the nude, with decorative objects such as collars, bands, tiaras, or cuffs being the only exceptions.

- Use of chastity cage or other means of erotic sexual denial.

- Wearing of external signs of "ownership" such as a collar.

- Having friends, family, or strangers aware of or witnessing one's treatment.

- Erotic objectification, where the bottom is cast in the role of an object, such as a footstool. Assuming the position of a man table on all fours or acting like a mute, sitting in a corner.

Sexual role-playing may or may not involve humiliation. For example, some people might play the part of a dog because they enjoy being mock forced into it and will emphasize the lowness of the bottom's status as an animal, whereas others might play the role of the dog without any element of humiliation, simply as an expression of their inner animal or playful spirit.

Psychology of Humiliation

Humiliation generally touches strong emotional buttons, especially when it becomes sexualized. Due to this, consent and paradoxically a high degree of awareness and communication is necessary to ensure that the result is desirable rather than abusive. For example, a submissive may enjoy being insulted in some ways, but genuinely crushed and devastated if humiliated or insulted in other ways.

Humiliation play is also connected to sexual fetishism, in which nonsexual activities may become sexualized by association with arousal, and also may be associated with exhibitionism in the sense of wanting others to witness the degradation. For some people, activities such as name-calling are a way of achieving ego reduction or getting over sexual inhibitions. This can be done in private or public. Some couples decide that when they are out shopping, your Queen may give you the order to sit, like a dog on the bench and wait for her. Or she may call you her slave or her pet.

As with all sexual activities, some people have sexual fantasies about humiliation, and others undertake it as a lifestyle or in a scene. Sexual fantasies of humiliation are very common, but for some people it is only done in private and as part of a fantasy. You and your Queen must be clear on what you are willing to do in private and public as well as places like sex clubs, resorts, and parties. Part of safe exploration is to be in agreement and for both of you to have given mutual consent.

CHAPTER 13
Physiological Effects of Femdom

Femdom is very exciting, and one of the effects on the body is a release of endorphins, which are responsible for happy feelings. The sensation of a hand hitting your skin can cause an adrenaline surge as additional blood flows to the surface, making all of the nerve receptors more sensitive, enhancing the sensation of a caress. The BDSM community refers to this as being a sensual experience, which shuts down the activity in your frontal cortex. It can be immensely helpful for overactive thinkers, which is why aggressive type A male personalities enjoy this. It almost calms them down.

On a physiological level, the fear element gets the adrenal glands going, flooding the system with epinephrine, followed by endorphins. Epinephrine, also known as adrenaline, energizes us when we are in the thick of "danger." Once we know the danger is over, the endorphins kick in. These are the body's natural painkillers, and they model opioids in how they make us feel by relaxing us and giving us a sense of calm and well-being.

A study from 2009 found that couples who engaged in positive, consensual sadomasochistic activity had lower levels of the harmful stress hormone cortisol and also reported greater feelings of relationship closeness and intimacy after their sexual play. They found that consensual BDSM can reduce anxiety by bringing the mind to an altered "flow" state of consciousness. This is similar to the feeling some get when they experience a "runner's high."

Subspace is a peaceful and somewhat hypnotic state that comes from the absolute surrender of the human will. Subspace is experienced when men surrender everything to the Queen.

When a woman dominates a man, be it physical domination or mental domination, there is an energy and a power that she has over him. There is also an energy exchange that demands submission. When a man surrenders to this power coming from the female, he enters into the submissive zone, which is the subspace. As he lets go and yields himself to the woman guard and allows his submissive nature to be expressed. This causes him to enter that tranquil and near hypnotic state. That is what is known as subspace. Subspace is a place of absolute surrender and a place where the female rules supreme. It is a magical place. It is powerful and it is beautiful. Only a man who surrenders his will to a woman and enters the submissive zone can fully see a woman in all her beauty and glory.

From attraction to action, sexual behavior takes many forms. At least for humans, this most basic of activities is anything but basic. As the pioneering sex researcher Alfred Kinsey put it, the only universal in human sexuality is variability itself. People normally engage in sexual activity for any number of reasons — to feel alive, to maintain a vital aspect of human functioning, to feel desirable and attractive, to achieve closeness, or to please a partner they love. Spanking adds an element of adventure and excitement to a routine sex life. The pleasure of sex arises from many factors including the release of neurochemicals, such as oxytocin and dopamine, which flood the system during orgasm, as well as the sense of connection communicated by touching.

According to Dr. Becky Spelman, a psychologist and clinical director of the Private Therapy Clinic, the reason for our appreciation of spanking is both physical and emotional. Classical conditioning is the automatic response to prior learning. For example, the experience can be linked to something you've experienced in the past. Dr Spellman says, "It usually occurs around a particular traumatic episode, which is then stamped into the child's psyche."

Something like spanking can cause a lot of shame in childhood, and rather than holding on to the shame, it's common for people to later in life turn the traumatic experience into a sexual one to help cope with what they have experienced, leading to a strong emotional connection between spanking and sex, which now manifests as a Femdom fetish.

When we're stressed or in pain, our brains release numerous chemicals: endorphin, serotonin, melatonin, epinephrine, norepinephrine, and dopamine. And not just physical pain but emotional and social discomfort as well — all for the purpose of rebalancing our bodies and trying to make us feel good again. One of the key players is dopamine, which is present in the body during pain and pleasure. Many agree this might be one of the reasons we can combine pain and pleasure in a single situation.

After the initial opiate-like euphoria wears off, many subs feel what's often called a "drop" or a "subdrop" The biochemicals begin to taper off, leaving a sleepy, relaxed feeling in their place. At this point, "aftercare," in which both of your physical and emotional needs are addressed, is crucial. After the exertion of play, for instance, a blanket or robe may be needed since the body temperature often drops from the sudden stoppage of energy. A Femdom activity like being restrained and spanking on the butt is thrilling because of its proximity to the sex organs, intensifying the overall sexual feeling. During spanking, the gluteal muscles are often squeezed together, which researchers have found is similar to what happens during orgasm. Sexual peaks are achieved when blood flow increases and collects in key hot spots or erogenous zones.

In the case of the male, the proximity of the buttocks to the scrotum and the penis is an important factor and seems to contribute to the erection. Blood rushing to the spanked bottom causes the male sexual organs to swell, much as they do in preparation for the orgasm. An additional anatomical element in sexual response to spanking is the fact that the anal opening shares some muscles with the perineum—a very erogenous area between the anus and the genitalia. During the course of most spankings, this area comes into contact with either the hand or the tool used to strike the buttocks.

Occasionally, depending on the size of the paddle or spanking implemented, the sexual organs will be accidentally struck — this can happen with either gender as the recipient. While no damage is sustained, an immediate sexual response is often the result. One phenomenon is the apparent fact that the sexual feelings induced by a spanking are either stronger than or blot out the presence of pain. Although there may be some physical discomfort, it adds to the eroticism of this activity, rather than detracting.

The emotional and psychological aspects of pain and pleasure involve submission, humiliation, sexual objectification, and role-playing. What you both experience in Femdom is the power dynamic or rush, in fantasy and reality, and it gives your Queen a certain power — the power to hurt, humiliate, heal, or stimulate.

Dominance is traditionally considered a male prerogative, so it is most popular among young men who are relatively powerless in real-life society — perhaps by choice, though usually they may not even have any testosterone-pumping energy. But more and more women are admitting that they enjoy being dominant and in complete control of men. Freud thought women had penis envy, which could be at the heart of why pegging with the strap-on dildo has become a favorite accessory of many dominant women. It's more likely that pegging places the woman in the control position and now men are able to experience how women feel, as the submissive.

Often as subtle as it is predictable, desire is part biology, part psychology, and takes shape differently in men and women. For men, arousal typically precedes desire. But for women, desire precedes arousal, in response to physical intimacy, emotional connection, and an atmosphere free of distractions and everyday concerns. Scientists are continuously exploring the interplay of biological influences, such as neurohormones that suppress or enhance desire, and psychological influences, such as emotions and relationships. Spanking is an example of a Femdom activity that affects a man's arousal, which leads to more desire of his Queen to control him, which eventually also leads to both being more turned on.

Besides so-called disciplinary, erotic, and sensual spanking, there is also therapeutic spanking, or "spanking therapy," which is employed for its curative effects. The therapeutic power of a spanking or flogging may be primarily physical, like a good massage or brisk rubdown. However, spanking therapy can also be deeply psychological, releasing the man being spanked from all kinds of stress, guilt, shame, and tension, with much of it stemming from childhood. The best spanking therapy breaks through destructive, debilitating mental and sexual blocks, improving the mental well-being of both the man getting spanked and his Queen.

In 2005, a team of Russian scientists led by Sergei Speransky found "whipping therapy" to be an effective prophylaxis against alcohol and drug abuse, depression, suicidal thoughts, and psychosomatic diseases due to the release of endorphins during and after spanking. Dr. Speransky recommends 30 sessions of 60 whip lashes on the buttocks in every session for maximum therapeutic effect. Today, the Queen spanking her man even during sex can serve as therapy. All of this is to demonstrate the powerful effects that Femdom activities can have on your physiology and well-being.

CHAPTER 14
Relationship Discipline

Relationship discipline is the practice in which the dominant, the Queen, sets rules that the submissive, the man, is expected to obey. When rules of expected behavior are broken, punishment is often used as a means of discipline. Discipline is one of the foundations of BDSM, but today it has made its way into many other types of relationships, including Female Led Relationship. In relationship discipline, rules can be made so that a submissive knows how they should behave and ensure the dominant is not displeased. Rules can also be for reminding subs of their inferior status or for training a novice sub.

When such rules are broken, punishment is often used as a means of discipline. Punishment itself can be physical, such as spanking or psychological, such as public humiliation or a combination of both. The goal of discipline is to teach the sub that they have made a mistake so that they learn self-restraint and become a better sub in the future. The punishment is generally related to the mistake and is generally proportional to the severity and frequency of the mistake. Punishments done on the submissive are for disciplining, in response to violations of predetermined rules, or for otherwise displeasing the dominant. Punishment is considered necessary to change the behavior, as a sub may repeat mistakes without it.

Discipline is not abuse. It is always done with your consent. In a "fun" scenario, this could play out in a scene in which you've been "naughty" and your Queen has to administer some sort of punishment like a spanking, time-out in the corner or an hour in a cage for more intense versions of Femdom. This is a type of punishment, for mutual enjoyment and entertainment. It is an act of mischievous play, a reward of pleasurable attention by engaging in an activity that is enjoyable to both. Contrast this to something that is more serious, real punishment is rarely enjoyable for either the submissive or the dominant, but which may be necessary.

Punishment is a tool used to adjust the submissive's behavior to a more desired state or outcome. You and your Queen decide how far to take your exploration of punishment. I like to explain what the punishment for certain transgressions will be and the sub is often allowed to agree or disagree. This encourages the idea of consent.

Part of relationship discipline is the use of a contract. A contract is an easy and uniform way for a submissive and dominant—even people who have never met before—to establish protocol, boundaries, and safety within a scene. Although it might seem silly or even like overkill to those who are new to relationship discipline and BDSM, using a contract can make it easier for you to exchange information that would prove an otherwise awkward conversation. A contract helps you and your man to decide on what is allowed and not allowed in the relationship and what the consequences are for breaking the contract. It may also include establishing a safe word and clearly defining what you both want.

Some examples include the Queen to be addressed as "My Queen" or the Sub will do the dishes every night or make the bed. During sex, everything will be allowed except anal sex or no more than ten lashes during spanking. A light contract can be used to ensure both of you adhere to the rules. I can recall walking into my friend's study and seeing a board up on the wall with her and her husband's name. Written under the names were their respective duties that were ticked off each day. In essence, my friend had created a type of contract that clearly outlined what was expected.

Relationship Discipline Involves Three Specific Parts:

- **Correction**. Taking time out to discuss the delay in assignment, the nature of the challenge/resistance, how to get past it, setting a new deadline and expectations. This requires clear communication and investment of time so that you are setting the submissive for success. Correction has three main parts (1) building awareness, (2) providing education, (3) framing the consequence or outcome.

- **Discipline.** Discipline focuses on a challenging task that will build or focus on a new skill for development. May include areas such as developing self-control, personal accountability, better communication, deeper understanding, etc. These usually come in the form of an exercise, drills, or a challenge that is actively watched and coached by the dominant partner. It may also be removal of a privilege that is providing a distraction. Discipline builds on a prior correction (which is a necessary component) and adds to it with practical and focused effort.

- **Punishment.** It is often a punitive experience that is the consequence for failing to execute or obey. Ideally, however, a punishment given is meant to override the cognitive mind and speak to the subconscious or primal mind directly, usually by associating the negative behavior/action with a negative consequence. These consequences often take the form of removal of unrelated privileges, denials of requests, subjection to discomfort, pain, humiliation, etc. This is the price or cost of disobedience, stubbornness, etc.

- **Punishment as an ordeal.** Punishment also serves as a physical start and end to a problem. When used as an ordeal, the punishment is given to allow the subject to move on without carrying mental or emotional burden. Some subs or slaves will carry a mistake with them, invisibly beating themselves up. Others will expect a harsh punishment, and if not given, will constantly anticipate it "at any time," By using punishment as an ordeal, it can create a firm and tangible break between what happened Before and After. This allows the sub to leave the past in the past and move forward knowing punishment is done and over with.

Both you and your Queen must decide on what the punishments will be. Many people will frown upon the use of these tactics, but relationship discipline has transformed relationships because both people are 100 percent present. Sexual fantasy and desire are another reason why couples will sometimes add discipline and Femdom activities into their relationship. Often the man and his Queen may view the disciplinary process as merely a prelude to sex or part of sex.

One important way to add discipline to the sexual routine and make it is so that you focus on her sexual fulfillment is to perform oral sex on her until satisfied. The reason this is an excellent way of adding discipline is because you're both motivated to do it and she gets some enjoyment from administering this type of discipline while being on the receiving end of her own pleasure.

Queens love this because it is often in bed or during sex that many women first indulge their desires to take charge. Other than this, the Queen will need to identify the best times to discipline and do training that does not coincide with sex. This is where the addition of chores, spanking, or removal of privileges may be of use. These are all topics that you and your Queen must discuss and come to an agreement.

Femdom and Transformational Discipline

When it is necessary to transform your partner and get more serious about femdom, you can use a Transformational Discipline. Transformational Discipline goes beyond normal Femdom activities and transforms the man. It is a type of punishment that creates some kind of quantum leap in his behavior, attitude, and understanding. It is a discipline that gives him a total emotional, spiritual, and moral makeover. There must be consent from him before you both decide to engage in this as it can bring about some deep changes.

A Transformational Discipline is intended to create genuine submission in the disciplined men. This is not the kind of submission that involves the man submitting only when it suits him to submit. This is the kind of submission that is lasting and genuine. A Transformational Discipline is also meant to teach him true obedience. Most couples enjoy this level of discipline with spanking, but the man generally will feel he needs it to completely submit to a woman in a Female Led Relationship. I have personally had many requests for this, but it is reserved for serious sessions.

A Transformational Discipline can be painful. This pain may consist primarily of physical pain. For example, the spanking that a man receives may be harsher and more severe than a normal punishment. On the other hand, a Transformational Discipline may also be painful because of its emotional content—due to the emotional experiences that the man has during his punishment. The physical punishment may not be any harsher than a normal punishment but the emotional effects of the discipline on the punished man may be deeper and longer lasting.

The need for Transformational Discipline arises when a man needs to be disciplined in a way that creates a significant change in his behavior and attitude, beyond what he normally experiences as a result of a regular punishment spanking. A Transformational Discipline becomes necessary when the Queen recognizes her man's need for a proper spanking that transforms his mind and heart. She seeks to teach him to become more positive and healthier in his outlook and comportment than he currently is. A man's misbehavior may be due to more than one cause. That is why a single spanking will not often be enough to cure a particular problem that the man has with his behavior or attitude. He may be disciplined one week for misbehavior and then must be punished again the following week for the same kind of disobedience, disrespect, or dishonesty.

It does not mean that he didn't learn his lesson from the first punishment. It simply means that the first one dealt with one aspect of his negativity in feelings or thoughts, which uncovered another problem that lay beneath. It has been previously explained that dealing with a man's repeated negative behavior or attitude is often like peeling an onion — the cause of his problem may be multi-layered. This multi-causal nature of some examples of feminine misbehavior is why it is often necessary to spank a woman for the same misbehavior on more than a single occasion.

Transformational Discipline is not necessarily designed to overcome this problem of the multi-layered causes of the man's misbehavior. It may work in this way, but it is not specifically intended to do so. The Queen must not attempt to accelerate his learning process too much by administering a Transformational Discipline just because she wants to speed things up.

The Queen will often get better results if she concentrates on giving one punishment at a time. Giving him a major session all at once in which he is unable to sit down for weeks will not work and can make the man unwilling to participate. If the Queen feels she has given him enough time to modify his behavior and attitude to be more positive, yet he still has not made the changes that she wants, then she is justified in administering a Transformational Discipline. The Queen must be patient with her man. If he does not make an effort to modify his behavior and attitude to more positive ways, she can use a Transformational Discipline. This will teach a man the true meaning of submission. He will learn not only to submit to her punishment but also to submit to his Queen.

The man in need of a Transformational Discipline will also usually have a strong need to be taught better obedience. The Transformational Discipline he receives will teach him obedience in a thorough and uncompromising way. He will learn to be more obedient to the Queen so that he has fewer problems of misbehavior in the future. He will learn obedience and especially the disciplinary process that his Queen initiates for his benefit.

A Queen needs to be consistent when she punishes her man for bad behavior. This means she needs to ensure he is always punished for any disciplinable offense he may commit. It means that he is always punished for bad behavior. If he breaks a rule or behaves in any manner that is dishonest, disrespectful, or disobedient to the Queen, then it follows that he should be disciplined for this masculine bad behavior. He must be punished.

Inconsistent punishment is when a man is allowed to get away with bad behavior. He may sometimes be disciplined for unruly behavior, but at other times, identical negative behavior or attitude may pass totally unpunished. This inconsistency will surprise the man. It may relieve the man if he has been afraid of being punished for his bad behavior. But the truth is, inconsistent punishment will disappoint and frustrate a man. One of the primary causes of increased masculine disobedience to his Queen is inconsistent punishment of his bad behavior. The Queen must always punish her man when he misbehaves. It is critical for his development as an obedient man that she does so.

If a man misbehaves, punishment must be automatic and swift. The best results occur when the man has to say what he is getting the spanking for. What is the transgression and what did he do to deserve the spanking? The Queen is free to use her lap, a counter, or standing to administer the spanking. It is worth noting that consistent punishment does not always mean immediate punishment. Some men incorrectly imagine immediacy equals consistency, and sometimes it can be much more productive for the Queen to inform him that his misbehavior will be dealt with later that day.

This leaves the man with the awareness that he is going to be reprimanded for his unruly behavior, and even thinking about his discipline will improve the way he acts. That's why a delayed punishment can have a better effect than an immediate punishment because the man has a lot of time to reflect on the spanking or whipping he will receive, as well as having a lot of time to reflect on what he did to deserve his upcoming chastising. Many men prefer to get their punishment over and done with because they realize the waiting period before the spanking is an additional discipline in itself.

Upkeep Discipline

Upkeep Discipline is one of the most important techniques used in Femdom. Upkeep Discipline has an incredible number of benefits for the man and for the couple. Among other things, Upkeep Discipline will act as a regular and frequent reminder to the man that he is subject to discipline by his Queen for his bad behavior. It will help to maintain his good behavior and good attitude. It will reduce the need for many punishment spankings since his behavior will tend to be better as a result of the Queen's Upkeep Discipline session.

The key to Upkeep Discipline is a regular schedule. The typical and recommended interval for Upkeep Discipline is once a week, but some Queens find that they need to use Upkeep Discipline every two or three days, or even daily. If a Queen has been giving her man a weekly Upkeep Discipline, it is normally important to keep that regular schedule in place to maintain consistency. If a scheduled Upkeep Discipline is missed, the woman's behavior and attitude will generally suffer, because the Queen's consistency has been damaged.

Since the key to Upkeep Discipline is regularity, anything that reduces or eliminates regularity will adversely affect the man and his behavior. It is critical to ensure that Upkeep Discipline is given regularly to men. When the Queen takes charge and makes great, well-thought-out decisions, it's easy for men to submit. Why? The woman has made the right call, and all he has to do is go along with her. A man needs consistency from his Queen because he needs to feel loved. When his Queen is inconsistent with any aspect of her female led discipline, he will begin to feel unloved. Of course, this is usually a misunderstanding of his Queen's motives. But according to the rules of masculine logic, his Queen doesn't love him if she fails to discipline him consistently.

It is important for his Queen to realize this and to make the connection between disciplining her man and his perception of whether she loves him or not. Giving him consistent discipline is giving him attention, which is a simple and effective way to remind him that the Queen is in charge and does love him. It shows she cares enough to discipline him for his bad behavior. A Queen who doesn't care at all about her man will simply let her do whatever he wants because she feels completely separate from him. She does not feel as though she has a shared destiny with him. But a Queen who cares for her man will discipline him for his own good since she wants what is best for him, even if she must bring him to tears in the process.

Being in a Female Led Relationship where the Queen is consistent gives a great feeling of emotional security to a man. The moral courage and strength that his Queen displays every time he is disciplined for bad behavior is a sign that she is strong enough to lead him. And as you know, a man's worst enemy is himself. When a Queen has been loving and kind enough to provide him with the deep emotional security that comes from living the female led lifestyle, she needs to be aware of what she has given him. If she suddenly becomes inconsistent with her discipline, he will feel the painful loss of this emotional security. He will feel lost and lonely. He will feel as though he exposed his innermost need for discipline to her, but that she has retreated from her promise to stand firm against his bad masculine behavior. Additionally, she has retreated from her promise to punish him whenever he misbehaves.

Consistent discipline is also necessary because it reduces or eliminates the man's juvenile behavior. A man behaves like a juvenile when he feels his Queen is not committed to the female led lifestyle, or when he wants to test her resolve, or for other different reasons. But consistency is an important part of preventing juvenile behavior because the man is always taught that he is responsible for his actions and words, and his Queen will consistently punish any misbehavior with spanking or even more harsh discipline. There is no need for this kind of childish male behavior. It is a form of testing, and if his Queen consistently disciplines him for bad behavior, it will remove any doubt in the man's mind. However, a lack of consistency is not an excuse for juvenile male behavior. It may be a contributing factor in juvenile behavior, but it is not an excuse for such misconduct.

One of the most important reasons for consistency is that it simply reduces all forms of bad masculine behavior. A consistent approach to discipline will reduce disobedience. It sounds rather obvious but is worth restating because many men are quite indignant about their Queen's apparent lack of consistency. Sometimes a man can focus more on his Queen's inconsistency rather than his own masculine misbehavior that arises as a result of it. But misbehavior is the most severe consequence of inconsistent approaches to a female led discipline of a man in which the primary goal of the punishment is to deal with misbehavior. It has other benefits, but that is the single most crucial one. A lack of consistency will result in a higher incidence of masculine disobedience, disrespect, and dishonesty.

As one might also expect, a lack of consistency also results in significantly greater disharmony in the Female Led Relationship. A firm and reassuring framework of female led discipline provides help for a man who is lost or damaged. Consistency is optimal. Male misbehavior tends to tear and attack the harmony and peace between a loving FLR couple. While it is the man's misbehavior that causes this negative impact, it is also the Queen's lack of consistency that has allowed the bad masculine behavior to surface.

CHAPTER 15
Rules in Femdom

F emdom and a female led lifestyle involves setting up some rules for a man's behavior that his Queen can monitor. If you break a rule, you will be disciplined for doing so. This discipline teaches men to behave in a more submissive, obedient, and loving way. Some couples set up rules together, while others rely on the Queen alone to create them. Some rules may be suggested by the man since he wants to work on some negative aspect of his own behavior or attitudes that he believes is holding him back from becoming a more submissive and loving man.

Some couples write down the rules, while others are quite happy to keep them on a purely verbal basis of agreement. Some men may have a tendency to debate the Queen's rules when they are called out for breaking them. This is not considered good behavior and can be disrespectful to the Queen. The most critical point is consistency. If you both as a couple decide to use light spanking when the man misbehaves, then the Queen must follow through with the punishment, and the man must obey.

Inconsistent rules are not normally a huge problem in female led households. The Queen cannot be unreasonable, but if it is agreed on, then both must follow through. Many couples find it fairly simple and straightforward to agree on a consistent set of rules for his behavior. These rules may change and develop over time. They may be added or subtracted as needed and dictated by common sense. A Queen must create consistent consequences for his man's unruly behavior. This simply means that a Queen may spank a man briefly for a minor offense, but she may whip a man to tears for a more serious offense, ensuring he is sobbing repentantly by the end of his punishment.

The amount and severity of the actual punishment may vary because the Queen may need to adjust these based on the man's attitude, but the relative outcomes must be consistent. Removal of privileges or light spanking for a very minor offense, and heavy paddling with tears or intense chores to be completed for a more serious offense. The consequences for different types of bad behavior must be consistent, even if they are not identical.

Delivering consistent consequences for male bad behavior is about maintaining the relative differences between offenses, so that it is always clear what the reason is for the punishment according to the seriousness of his unruly behavior. He should know that if he gets a light spanking for an insignificant offense, he will get a severe whipping for a serious offense. Enforcing rules will be an important responsibility of the Queen. Identify behaviors like disrespect, topping from the bottom, bratting, and constantly refusing to complete tasks as requested as major infractions for which training will be needed.

Specific Rules of Conduct

Addressing the Queen

- You will address the Queen as "My Queen."

- You will always ask multiple times throughout the day, such as "How may I help?"

- If she wants to discuss something, you will make yourself immediately available by listening only without interjecting.

- You must allow the Queen to speak, and you will speak only when she has given you permission.

Daily Routine

- You will await the return of your Queen either in proper position or at the dining room or living room.

- You will be naked on command or in underwear if that's what she chooses, otherwise you will be properly groomed.

- You will complete all chores from your list provided or what has been discussed.

- You will tend to the children as needed.

- Your man cave and other areas of the house you frequent must be in orderly shape daily.

- You will not be allowed to remain locked in your man cave or play video games without the Queen's permission.

- If you are watching TV, ask your Queen what she wants to watch.

- Breakfast must be prepared before she rises.

- You must draw the Queen's bath if she desires this so that it's prepared for her before she is ready to take one.

- You will do turndown service on your bed, which is neatly made each day.

- Feel free to bow when you greet or address your Queen.

Dining Out

- You will pull the chair out for your Queen to make sure she is seated before you sit.

- You will not be allowed to look at your phone at the dinner table.

- You will ensure your Queen has a menu and allow her to decide what she wants to order.

- She can either order for you or you can choose whatever you like.

- You will refrain from looking around or commenting about other women in public.

- Your eyes remain on the Queen at all times.

- Elbows will remain off the table, and you must sit upright at all times.

- Knife in right hand, fork in left hand.

In Public

- You walk two steps behind the Queen or with her, but never in front of her.

- You address the Queen as "My Queen" at all times.

- You will not gawk, stare, or comment about other women in the Queen's presence.

- You do not offer commentary unless she expressly requests it.

- You will open doors where at all possible for your Queen.

- You will help your Queen carry heavy packages at all times.

You must never be derogatory or joke or speak about any private matter in public.

CHAPTER 16
Create the Perfect Femdom Session

The purpose of the session is to help create the perfect Femdom sex life. The following are only tips and guidelines to enhance your experience with your Queen. Though it may be based on ideas from BDSM and Femdom, it will not be the professional methods used by pros in these areas. The idea is to add some elements to your own life and customize them to suit your needs.

What makes a Femdom session so intense is for your Queen to keep you, the submissive, on edge: scared and horny. You will be so excited with anticipation and aroused, so it's important to have time to explore and be relaxed. This is a great way to explore your desires. Your Queen can add many contrasting sensations, anticipation and introducing rules and rituals to guide you to the meditative subspace.

The simplest way to do this is to wait in submission. Waiting is the purest form of submission, and it is also a very calming state to be in. During this time, you can relax and get into that space, ready for their punishment, or whatever their dominant has planned for them.

One of the reasons bondage and being restrained is so powerful is that it helps build the excitement and you can relax and surrender to whatever your Queen desires. Being tied down or restrained can actually be quite freeing, as it liberates the submissive from guilt, shame, or anxiety surrounding their masochistic desires.

When you engage with your Queen in BDSM and Femdom, especially in the bedroom, this is called "the session." There are some general rules to follow so you can make it methodical and more intense than your normal sexual interactions. You always want to set the mood and create a sexy atmosphere. Maybe even have a lovely dinner, do some flirting, then go to your room or living room to worship your Queen. It is extremely important to make these sessions very sexy, with a slow build up and be pleasurable.

Turn off your phones, put the kids to sleep or get a babysitter, and leave the pets out of the space. There should be no distractions. Turn off the TV. This is your time to not only focus on increasing the intensity of your sessions but also make worshipping your Queen a ritual and a priority. Perhaps this is the night you will be allowed out of chastity, or maybe it's learning some new techniques, or a discipline session with your Queen. Ensure that all of your tools, toys, and costumes are laid out, along with lube, towels, and tissues. You don't want to have to go searching for these items in the middle of your love session.

A fun idea throughout the year would be to add to your existing space, such as sex furniture, a sex swing, cross, paddles, ticklers, and more. The great thing about Femdom sessions is that Surrendering is about letting all of that go. It provides a sense of catharsis by creating a safe space in which both dominant and submissive can escape the outside world and focusing solely on each other.

Surrendering to someone else, like your Queen, creates one of the strongest psychological bonds you can have with another person. If you and your Queen are trying to make your connection stronger, you must start to understand the mind of the other. Then you can explore subspace and new levels of pleasure and pain.

Getting Started

Generally, the Queen will instruct you to start by taking a shower and get dressed in the outfit of her choice or maybe she wants you naked. You may want to have your collar or cuffs ready so your Queen can restrain you or lead you around if she desires. The Queen wears whatever she wants. Leather, lace, boots, or high heels and hosiery.

Greet Your Queen

You may bow or kneel until called forward. You can approach crawling or wait for her to approach you. You and your Queen should decide how you want to greet each other. This can extend to daily greetings as well. Some Queens require the sub to kiss her shoe, boot, hand. Some Queens want the sub to crawl around a bit or perform some other gesture of greeting. Some couples enjoy the Queen being on her throne while the man can approach and kneel or bow for the greeting. He can say things like, "My Queen, I'm here to serve you."

The Queen should be encouraged to speak firmly to you and express her desires. She can say things like, "I command you." and "You will worship only me." When the Queen becomes accustomed to instructing and giving you commands, she begins to sense her power over you, and you can experience the feeling of being dominated. If kneeling is too hard on your joints, you can sit in a chair upright and attentive or simply bow.

Some variations to this greeting may include you waiting in a corner until the Queen calls you, remaining blindfolded until the Queen approaches and removes the cloth from your eyes, or you are waiting in a cage until your Queen allows you out. The ideas are extensive on what you can experience. However, ensure that whatever you both decide to do there is agreement from both of you on all aspects.

At this time, the Queen can place a collar on you and lead you around the room, or she may lead you to the bed where she can restrain you or do whatever she likes to prepare you to serve her. Maybe she wishes to flog you first, or keep you blindfolded and tickle you, or attempt some facesitting before you begin. She decides. She may instruct you to give her a massage or begin to massage her feet to get her warmed up. You are then free to move into aspects of foreplay, massaging her body, leading right into oral pleasure where you make your Queen's orgasm the center of your lovemaking before your own.

Bad Behaviors Are Not Permitted

Men sometimes in the beginning try to instruct the Queen on what he wishes for. This type of bad behavior is topping from the bottom. The man, who is the sub, is attempting to get the Queen to do what he wants. This should not occur.

Yes, you can discuss with your Queen things you may enjoy, but ultimately, the decision to do anything is hers during the scene. The Queen needs to firmly stop this kind of behavior and there may be punishments and discipline issued for it.

Other examples of bad behavior would be failing to greet the Queen correctly, not finishing chores, failing to execute a ritual correctly, disrespecting the Queen by raising your voice, and engaging in arguments and gawking at other women when you are out in the presence of your Queen. You and your Queen can make a list of the behaviors that are not allowed, and she may choose to punish and discipline you for them since you've been a bad boy.

The Queen's Language

How the Queen issues commands and instructions can be very arousing, and this should be incorporated into the session as much as possible. She can say things like, "You are now my slave, my submissive. You serve only one Queen. You may now greet me." Or "I command you as my good loyal slave and subject you to lick my boot, or crawl around on all fours, or make the sound of a donkey. Your Queen commands you."

Or, during chastity, when your Queen is putting on the chastity cage, she can say, "Now I own you completely, all of you. Your cock is only to serve me." And you answer, "My Queen, my body and I exist to serve your every desire." It is best to experiment with different words and language to determine what works best. Make it fun, sexy, and exciting.

The Femdom Daily Experience

Female Led Relationships are about lifestyle and the daily interaction, and there are basic rules for how you, the supportive gentleman, need to execute every day. Femdom allows couples to take the daily experience to a whole new level of excitement by introducing new routines.

When you return home, remove your clothing from being out and working, take a shower, and dress for Queen worship. This can be your leather pants, shorts, shirt or pajamas or maid's uniform. Your Queen will dictate what she prefers you to wear.

You will look presentable. You can go about doing your chores like cleaning, cooking, and taking care of the kids. Before the Queen arrives home, the table should be set with her favorite wine or snack.

When the Queen comes home, you help remove her coat, boots, etc., and you wait for her to attend dinner. Perhaps you have your favorite night routine of sitting down to dinner as a family, but once this is over, it is time for Queen worship.

You draw her a bath or prepare your bed, or sex room, for titillating activities if that is what she desires. It is your duty to ask her, "My Queen what do you desire tonight? "Maybe she's tired and just wants an hour of you massaging her feet or rubbing her neck. Maybe she wants to massage you. Or maybe she wants a sexy shower or bubble bath together. The point is, she needs to make the rules on what will go on that night. Perhaps it's a night of play where you'll be inviting over a Bull or swinging with another couple — you must know what is going to be happening, so you, as the supportive gentleman, can get things ready. You may want to lay out her sexy nightie, garter, or her leather outfits, sex toys, and tools. It is your responsibility to prepare.

CHAPTER 17
Types of Femdom Play

T he following are several activities you can explore as part of Femdom play. It is important for you and your Queen to agree to the rules and give mutual consent. Establish safe words and discuss limits and boundaries. Here are some popular forms of Femdom play.

Spanking or Impact Play

Spanking is a popular activity in BDSM and Femdom, and it allows the Queen to take full control of her man and issue punishment and discipline if necessary. There are many aspects to explore with spanking and many different toys and tools to add for variety. The Queen must always be aware of your limits and all safe words must be established.

Anal Play

Anal play can involve the use of dildo strap-ons, butt plugs, and more. It's a very popular part of Femdom, but it may be new for vanilla couples transitioning to more intense and extreme forms of play.

Spanking tables and spanking racks are great for these types or you merely lying on the bed. Now, depending on what you and your Queen's experience level is and what you have agreed on, proceed with anal play slowly. You must be warmed up properly with plenty of foreplay.

The Queen may get very excited to try a dildo or pegging, and if you're new, it may take some time to adjust. Pegging and anal play allows you to experience role reversal. What does it feel like for her to be in control of the sexual activities? She is immediately given the feeling of what it's like to lead the sex and be in complete control of you. Let's face it, as a sub, there is no other better submissive position than you lying on your stomach rendered helpless and unable to move. The other reason this position is so exciting is you can hear her but you can't see her, and the thrill of the anticipation of what could happen is so exhilarating you may not be able to control yourself.

Bondage

Bondage is use of physical restraints for erotic stimulation. When your Queen ties you up, you are immediately given the feeling of helplessness, excitement, arousal, and adventure. She can do whatever she wants to you. There are proper methods for doing bondage, so it's important to learn these skills if you plan on doing this regularly. The easiest way to begin is using ankle and wrist restraints. Tying limbs to bedposts can be a great way to begin bondage.

Who can resist the scene when Sharon Stone ties up Michael Douglas with a silk scarf in the movie *Basic Instinct* in what could be the greatest sex scene in film history? Restraints are a very sexy way for the Queen to show ultimate control over you.

Torture

An example of torture is cock and call torture. This is where your Queen would tie up your penis and testicles, demonstrating that she has you under complete control because she controls your manhood which is considered to be the most important part of a man's body. As the sub, you are rendered helpless. The arousal comes with the power play. You cannot help but surrender to a woman who literally has you by the cock and balls.

It's very important to start with light restraints to not put excessive pressure on your testicles, which are very delicate. You can also add other forms of bondage, like tying hands, legs, and other limbs for added excitement.

Fetishes

A fetish is sexual attraction and arousal from an object or nonsexual body part. Fetishes can be very diverse from an attraction to feet, hosiery, leather, latex, high heels, and more. Fetish play can serve as wonderful foreplay for you and your Queen to explore. Maybe you like the sight of her heels or her paddle. Spend some time exploring these desires.

Foot fetish is a very popular fetish in which men enjoy the sight, smell, and feel of women's feet on them and even on their face. Another one is shoe fetish, and the men will kneel and kiss his Queen's boot or shoes or enjoy the off heel digging into his leg or back. Remember, there must always be care when exploring these types of activities.

Pet Play

Pet play is just as it is described—you dress up like a pet dog, donkey, or cat, complete with ears and tail and spend some time acting out scenarios. Some couples love to take it further where you eat out of your dog bowl, and you are taken for a walk on a leash. Of course, your Queen is your owner, and you can do a variety of tricks for her enjoyment. Some couples get very aroused with this type of play because it is so different from all others.

Tease And Denial

Teasing and denial are similar to what occurs in chastity. The slave is forbidden to orgasm until his Queen permits him. Teasing can happen throughout sex. You get aroused and brought to the point of wanting to come, but you must hold it back and calm it down until the Queen instructs you to come. Use of the chastity cage over days or weeks can be incorporated into this type of chastity play, but the idea is that by removing your focus from your own orgasm and focusing all of your energy on your Queen, you build willpower, and you learn to serve her better. You should incorporate more oral sex and foreplay to increase the intensity and sexual arousal of chastity.

The Rack

When you are ready to elevate your Femdom to new levels, you can add great pieces like a cross, rack, or bench. Your Queen will tie you to one of these and do with you whatever she wants to. The feel of the furniture makes the arousal even more intense. This is what makes the setting for domiantrixes so intense. The furniture, lighting, instruments, and décor all play a role in creating the right mood, which you can do at the comfort of your home.

Role-Playing

Role-playing can be as common as doctor and patient or teacher and student. Role-playing is a common aspect of BDSM "play." It may involve two or more people who "act out" a particular scene or fantasy. BDSM role-play can happen in person or virtually. It almost always involves at least one individual being dominant and another being submissive. It may be simple, or it may be complicated enough to require a script. And actual sex is not the focus. The roles are acted out in a particular scene or fantasy. You are the submissive, while your Queen is the dominant. You can create as you go along or have scripts in place.

BDSM

For BDSM to be real, it must involve an exchange of power with a lot of trust and respect. The couple has to decide which role they want to play, the dominant one or the submissive, and it's that dynamic that creates erotic intensity.

BDSM Common Forms of BDSM Play:

- Bondage (restraint or restriction)

- Wax (dripping hot wax on the skin)

- Impact (spanking, slapping, caning, flogging)

- Sensation (using tools, such as feathers, a paddle, burlap, on the skin)

- Sensory deprivation (blindfolds, earmuffs, ear plugs)

Queening or Facesitting

Facesitting, also known as queening or kinging, is a sexual practice in which one partner sits on or over the other's face, typically to allow oral to genital contact or oral to anal contact. It is often included in Femdom as the Queen can show her superiority and dominance while you are in a very submissive position to serve her. Sex is for the Queen's pleasure is the first rule in FLR, so Queening is basically your Queen in complete control over you while you orally pleasure her.

The Queening stool is a low seat that fits over your face and contains an opening to allow oral-genital and/or oral-anal stimulation of your Queen while she is seated atop. This tool is particularly useful because all of the pelvic floor, vagina, and anal muscles relax, and you can feel comfortable that you won't be smothered. Queening is so much more enjoyable when you and your Queen are comfortable. Facesitting allows for direct stimulation of the vagina or the anus and the feeling of power for the Queen can dramatically increase sexual arousal and sexual gratification.

The basics are very simple. Have your Queen hover above your face or use a Queening stool. Once she is positioned, she is slowly riding your face without smothering you. You are using your tongue to give her the best pleasure. My book *Oral Sex for Women* provides incredible techniques to keep this activity exciting and to give her the best orgasm of her life.

Queening is mandatory in your Femdom relationship. It's a great way for you to experience her control of you while you're completely restrained, helpless, and submissive, which will help you to become much more devoted in your servitude.

CHAPTER 18
Pegging

P egging is becoming a very popular activity for couples wishing to explore Femdom. While it is not for everyone and does not have to be part of a Female Led Relationship or female led marriage, it is an exciting activity for women and men since there is an incredible power exchange that takes place, and the mental stimulation exceeds any rush provided by physical pleasure. It makes for great sexual foreplay as the Queen can feel her power when she puts on the strap-on and asserts her dominance.

Women find pegging liberating for the social statement that it makes. Strap-on play strips the man of his masculinity and macho ways and causes the man to surrender his strength and his will over to his Queen. A woman will sense you giving up resistance and submitting to her. This is an incredible power rush to the woman. Also, the effects of this activity usually last for some time. The man who submits to this activity won't have any desires to take charge around his dominant wife. After the activity, he is usually meek and submissive to her outside of the bedroom.

Strap-on play is a power exchange, yet some may think it's about women wanting to be men. Quite the contrary — it's much more about role-playing and the empowering of women as they unleash another level of their previously dormant power. The submissive man is feeling a combination of sexual stimulation, discomfort, and humiliation during strap-on sex. I believe it also helps men to understand how women feel when "boys will be boys," and they feel they have to give it to a woman. It goes along with helping them build empathy and understanding of what the Queen has to experience and helps to train him in service.

Pegging also gives you a chance to experience how women feel all their lives. You can understand the nuances of submission and you show your ultimate acceptance of your Queen as your dominant leader when you submit to her desire to use a strap-on during sex. It can be added as foreplay or introduced at any point your Queen decides she wants to take the top position. It's important to start slow and warm up. Most anuses need to be eased into being penetrated. Lather the receiver's anus and the shaft of the dildo with lube until both are nice and slick. It's best for your Queen to start massaging on the outside of the butt and massage the ring of muscles around the anus.

Then, when you're ready, your Queen can use a well-lubed finger to penetrate you. The best technique is to start making circles inside the anus, then she can slowly thrust in and out. You must communicate how you feel throughout. Choose a strap-on made of medical grade silicon so it's hygienic and easy to clean after. The best position for pegging is probably doggy style. Your Queen should begin by pressing the tip of the dildo against your opening. Breathe in and exhale as she moves slowly deeper and deeper. Keep the mood sexy and go slow. Aftercare is very important and mandatory.

Pegging can be emotional for both you and your Queen, especially if it's your first time. Take time to relax, cuddle, and talk about feelings, hesitations, or concerns. Reassure each other that it's just healthy sexploration. Some questions to ask might be: How did it feel? What did you really like? What didn't you like? Which would you rather I skip next time? Is there anything we should do differently?

CHAPTER 19
Spanking and Impact Play

S panking has become one of the most popular activities in Femdom and is fast becoming a favorite pastime for many couples. Spanking is described as a common form of corporal punishment, involving the act of striking the butt or some other area of another person, to cause physical pain. More severe forms of spanking, such as switching, paddling, belting, caning, whipping, and birching, involve the use of an object instead of a hand. Spanking began in slavery and as part of the punishment of children.

There has been an outcry against spanking children today as researchers raise questions about the long-term psychological effects, so it is losing popularity with parents and occurs much less than before. But spanking is witnessing a rise in the bedroom, which is fast becoming one of the most popular additions to many couples' sex lives.

For years, spanking was depicted in movies when a man felt the need to control a woman he thought was out of control. There are film scenes showing a man grabbing his woman, throwing her over his leg and slapping her behind. Old episodes of *I Love Lucy* to the 2004 *Along Came Polly* depict this behavior, and even Justin Timberlake promised in his 2006 single "SexyBack," by singing "I'll let you whip me if I misbehave." Rihanna also sings about whips and chains in "S&M," and in the Netflix series *Weeds,* Nancy Botwin gets a good spanking from Esteban, the head of the cartel.

Today, particularly in the bedroom, the tides are turning, and men are being spanked by the women they now serve as their Queen. There is growing interest in spanking as more couples are engaging in it. Sex expert Sienna Sinclaire says, "Erotic spanking is all about spanking someone for sexual pleasure for both parties." The person being spanked enjoys it, and the person doing the spanking is also getting enjoyment. Spanking has become so popular that now there are thousands of products available on Amazon to ensure you can create the perfect spanking experience. But is spanking during sex a new concept? Apparently not.

Erotic spanking became extremely popular during the Renaissance where it was practiced openly in French courts. It also grew in popularity in Victorian England. More recently, erotic spanking gained international appeal in the 1940s in *Bizarre* magazine, which published illustrated fetish stories and articles. In the 1970s, spanking groups sprang up around the United States, many of which are still active today, such as Shadow Lane, Crimson Moon, and Paddles Club NYC, with the most famous retreats organized by spanking, BDSM, and fetish film director Carter Stevens. But some of the early depictions of spanking can be seen in ancient Egyptian and Italian art.

In spanking role-play, the Queen must administer a spanking for her man's disobedience. A fun way to do this is if you disrespect your Queen in any way, such as making fun of her, failing to listen to her or abide to her rules, then she can command you to stand up, pull down your pants, and give you a sweet spanking before leading to sex. Some couples enjoy just giving the spanking as daily discipline, others prefer to begin with the spanking, which can lead to being so turned on you must have hot passionate sex afterward.

Getting smacked on the butt was a real turn on for centuries, and many couples spank each other and give a little tap on the butt just for fun. You can see spanking or taps on the butt in sports as a gesture of support from a teammate. And, of course, there is no end to spanking references in movies like *Fifty Shades of Grey* in which it was definitely what Christian Grey enjoyed the most in his encounters with Anastasia Steele. After this film, spanking was thrust into the mainstream. Join any dominatrix group or watch any dominatrix videos and you'll realize spanking is one of the most requested activities by men. There is simply a great desire for men to experience being tied up or put over their mistress's knee to be spanked for bad behavior or fun.

Why has spanking become so popular? Our desire to engage in spanking comes out of our need for attention. The only time most children get attention is when their parents are disciplining them, and maybe as adults we crave this undivided attention. Though spanking children is not advisable and outlawed, spanking in the bedroom has skyrocketed. As the leader of the *Love & Obey* and Female Led Relationship movement, I have seen how spanking has particularly become popular with women spanking men. So, I will be exploring spanking as it pertains to fun displays of discipline and dominance in the relationship.

Though spanking comes out of BDSM, this book is in no way intended to instruct on the particular practices or customs of BDSM. The intention of this book is to focus on fun things the Queen can do to discipline her man in a playful respectful way if the man desires it and there is full consent. I will also touch lightly on spanking as a means of serious discipline for those couples who wish to learn more about this and, of course, how spanking can be added to as part of relationship discipline. Overall, spanking during sex is meant to add some variety and that element of fun and adventure to any relationship.

During one of the first parties I've ever attended for fetish, a massive gathering with thousands of people were moving through a maze of different rooms set up with everything to do with BDSM, bondage and torture. It was straight out of the movie *Eyes Wide Shut*. In one room, I observed an old man getting saran wrapped and strung up, hanging from the rafters. Three dominatrixes prepared themselves like a scene out of the movie *Wonder Woman* on the island of Themyscira where the female warriors prepared for battle. Then once they were armed with their floggers, they began to flog the man while we all watched. But what I cannot stop thinking about was the smile on his face. He urged them to beat him harder and more.

They would replace their floggers for riding crops, and no matter how hard they whipped the man, he just got happier and seemed to be in a state of ecstasy. This got me thinking about the idea of spanking in the bedroom and how both the fear of what it could be and the painful sensations wake up something primal in men and women. Something which cannot be achieved with any other sexual act. Men who want to be dominated are intensely turned on and the women derive a great deal of satisfaction from completely controlling her man.

Think of the intense excitement you will feel when your Queen ties you up, teases you to death with role-playing, ticklers, and light strokes of a whip. For some, this is a way of life. I know many couples who cannot wait to engage in some kind of dominance play and relationship discipline. Women have admitted to me the satisfaction they get when they can control their men, spank them whenever they want, and they have their men begging for more and treating them infinitely better than before.

Spanking can cause many of our deep desires for complete attention from our partners because, let's face it, you need complete, undivided attention when administering and receiving a spanking. It resolves many of the disrespectful behaviors that have arisen and are accepted by society as normal, but which can lead to the unraveling and the eventual destruction of the relationship.

How many times have I seen couples spending quality time together and they are on their phones or social media? Spanking in the bedroom is the one time a couple's minds do not wander, and you can't be on the phone. To partake in spanking and relationship discipline, there cannot be distractions, and this is one of the advantages to the relationship.

Within the world of dominance and submission, discipline is often eroticized and executed in a way society wouldn't otherwise condone. But many couples are waking up a dead sex life with the addition of spanking and light BDSM.

In the Female Led Relationships, more men have admitted that they enjoy and have a strong desire for their women to whip them and be aggressive. Hence, this book will deal with erotic spanking and how the Queen can administer this discipline to her man during sex. Today, more relationships are being led by women. Women are taking charge in the household and in the bedroom. Men love the experience of being under the spell and the dominance of women. Spanking just adds to the feeling of control for the Queen. When women feel empowered, they are at their best, and men get excited when they take charge and show their power. So, it's a win-win for most.

The popularity of spanking shows no signs of slowing down.

Spanking is fast becoming the favorite bedroom pastime and at 670,000 searches a month, it shows that its popularity worldwide is only growing. A recent survey showed that 75 percent of women and 66 percent of men enjoyed erotic spanking. This book will serve as an introduction to erotic spanking, and it will provide some fun ideas on how to add spanking to your sexual routine in a safe way. It cannot be understated that safety and consent are both crucial. This must always be a pastime between consenting adults who are in a committed relationship. Added to an already healthy sex life, spanking can be a fun way to spice up the bedroom while fulfilling your fantasies.

When a couple begins a female led lifestyle, they need to discuss how they want to move forward. Are they going to agree on a list of rules first, or will they agree that the female leader will train the man as she sees fit? Some couples prefer the former while others prefer the latter. Each individual couple must figure out what works for them. In my first book, *Love & Obey*, I used positive reinforcement behavioral training to encourage good behavior, and I do not endorse the use of non-consensual, physical punishment. Today, I still only endorse safe physical punishment, which is consensual and not harmful in any lasting or serious way. A couple must always fully agree before engaging in this practice and both should be adults.

I have come to see why spanking, paddling, whipping and caning is important and is such a popular and erotic form of training men, especially in a Female Led Relationship. If a Queen wishes to rule over a man, she must demand obedience. A Female Led Relationship may start out as a male sexual fantasy, but it must evolve into a real lifestyle in which the woman leads and the man obeys, or it simply will not work. Spanking and relationship discipline has the ability to be a fun pastime to your sexual routine, or it has the power to transform the relationship and increase intimacy and respect.

Today, in Female Led Relationships, many men enjoy being spanked by their Queens, and many have introduced it as an acceptable weekly—even daily—occurrence. Learning proper technique and ways to introduce it into the sex life is key. I will be discussing all aspects of erotic spanking, including the history, proper techniques, tools, and much more. The goal of this book is to help men and women engage in fun, healthy, safe, and consensual spanking as part of their sex routine. I will also add some information on the serious practice of relationship discipline and touch base again on BDSM.

It is my wish that all couples use this as a way to build more intimacy and spice up your sex life. A healthy, fun sex life can dramatically change your relationship for the better. Spanking is a pivotal part of the Female Led Relationship where the woman administers the spanking both for fun times as well as discipline. Being the leader of the *Love & Obey* movement, which promotes a healthy and safe female led lifestyle, spanking with consent from both the Queen and her man fits perfectly into the female led world. Women are already in charge and more than capable of giving a great spanking session. Spanking has the power to transform a relationship from dull, boring, monotonous and failing to exciting, intimate, and rewarding. Happy safe spanking.

CHAPTER 20
Why Is Spanking Such a Turn On?

Men have been known to crave fantasies of being dominated and women love powerful men. According to a study by a new paper published in the journal *Social Psychological and Personality Science* by Joris Lammers and Roland Imhoff, social power reduces inhibition. In other words, powerful, even wealthy, men are aroused by being dominated by women in bed. In one of the earliest episodes of the show *Game of Thrones*, Khaleesi is instructed to dominate her husband, played by Jason Momoa, after taking it from him. Once she does this, she is treated like a Queen and a Goddess.

However, another study claims that power frees people from their inhibitions, and thereby increases sadomasochistic thoughts in everyone, masochistic tendencies in men who are being hurt or tortured, and sadistic thoughts in women. So, this is the reason why men crave torture and are turned on when aggressive women do this, particularly during sex.

The findings of the study showed that power increases the arousal to sadomasochism. Furthermore, the effect of power on arousal by sadistic thoughts is stronger among women than men, while the effect of power on arousal by masochistic thoughts is stronger among men than women. Masochistic is defined as deriving sexual gratification from one's own pain or humiliation. As was uncovered, men crave physical torture from dominant women, and this coincides with my findings as well. Men simply love the pain felt when a powerful woman smacks them on the behind, and the powerful woman is turned on by doing the act.

A 2013 study found that both dominant and submissive practitioners of BDSM were less neurotic, more extroverted, more open to new experiences, more conscientious, and less sensitive to rejection. They also had higher subjective well-being compared to the control group. This could mean two things: People with these traits are attracted to kinky sex, or kinky sex can help you grow and gain confidence.

I always think of the scene from *The Wolf of Wall Street* where Jordan Belfort is so taken with his dominatrix Venice that he was caught calling out her name in his sleep. In the scene, Venice's preferred punishment is to pour candle wax on his butt while whipping him, and he enjoys it so much that he is dreaming about it. But Mr. Belfort, a powerful head of an investment firm, craved this activity despite having access to thousands of women from all walks of life in various sexual escapades, yet this is the one he dreams about.

There are many reasons as to why erotic spanking is exciting. First, there's the physical sensation. If done properly, spanking stimulates a person's genitals indirectly and creates a subtle sensation that is, no doubt, pleasurable.

On the other hand, there's the psychological aspect of it. Erotic spanking can also have a lot to do with role-play and pretend-punishment that flares up one's imagination and makes the sexual experience much more intense.

Spanking can allow people to begin experiencing BDSM in a fun way. Discipline in BDSM is the practice in which the dominant sets rules that the submissive is expected to obey. When rules of expected behaviors are broken, punishment is often used as a means of disciplining. In BDSM, rules can be made so that a submissive or sub knows how they should behave so that the dominant is not displeased.

In Femdom, this translates into men behaving properly according to the Queen's rules. Rules can also be for reminding subs of their inferior status or for training a novice sub. In BDSM, when such rules are broken, punishment is often used as a means of discipline. Punishment itself can be physical, such as caning, or psychological such as public humiliation or a combination of both—through bondage and spanking. So, spanking during sex extends from this practice of BDSM and discipline, which becomes a fun way for the Queen to exert her dominance over her man for both of their enjoyment.

What turns on one person about spanking is personal. Shelby Devlin, a sex and intimacy coach, says that the person getting spanked may love the feeling of powerlessness, while another person might only enjoy the physical sensation. So, when you first decide you want to explore spanking, she suggests taking time out for self-reflection. What is it about spanking that turns you and your partner on? Analyze it and discuss it.

Dawn Michael, a certified sexuality counselor and marriage and family therapist with a Ph.D. in human sexuality, says that being submissive or dominant with your partner can be a sexy role-play that spanking easily falls under. She says that "spanking can be a turn on for both a man and a woman who enjoy being submissive to their partner, working it into a role of submission to their Dom for a man or their master for a woman."

Men have always loved aggressive woman and spanking in sex offers the opportunity for women to take control and spice things up during sex. Imagine an entire foreplay session in which she ties you up, blindfolds you, and throws you down on the bed, and runs her flogger or horse whip all the way up from your toes to your head, then gives you a few slaps. Afterward, she gets on top and rides you to orgasm. Who can resist?

Almost everyone has some secret desire, fantasy, or fetish that turns them on in the bedroom or elsewhere. Some choose to keep their fantasies to themselves and think about them when they're alone. They consider this part of their sexuality unnecessary to share. However, others have a strong urge to share their fantasy or fetish, desiring to act it out with partners. Feelings of guilt, shame, and confusion about our fantasies and what turns us on are common in our society. What is often difficult for people to understand is that sexual awakening happens when we are children. Although childhood sexuality is a natural part of development, it is often ignored in our culture, shunned, or brushed under the rug as wrong. The child is made to feel ashamed or guilty for having sexual thoughts and desires. No explanations are given, and nothing is talked about.

CHAPTER 21
Tools for Spanking

There are various tools available that are considered the best for fun spanking sessions, including the hand, paddle, strap, hairbrush, cane, animal taming whip, and feather duster or belt. Other popular ones are riding crops, whips, switches, birches sneakers, phonebooks, rolled-up catalogs or newspapers, rulers, or martinets. Below we will discuss a few of these tools in detail.

The Paddle

A spanking paddle is one of the most popular tools for spanking. It is mostly used to strike a person on the buttocks as this has been found to be an erotic zone. The act of spanking a person with a paddle is known as "paddling." Paddles are made of wood or plastic. Paddles were used in schools for punishment, so people who like spanking may want that feeling of being disciplined. It is believed that the paddle may have originally been used for the punishment of slaves to cause intense pain without permanent damage.

The paddle makes its way into the sexual experience when the master uses it to spank the sex slave. This can be a man or a woman, but in the Female Led Relationship, the woman will often do the spanking and the man is the submissive. Different types of paddles will have different sensations. Rigid paddles will likely hurt less than many flexible paddles. Paddles made from faux fur are going to feel almost like a massage, while a paddle made from silicone, wood, or hard leather will provide an intense feeling.

It's probably best to start with light and progress to intense. A large paddle will probably feel less painful than a paddle that only strikes a concentrated area.

The Flogger

Floggers are great to use once you start with the paddle and you want to progress. One step past the paddles, you'll find the floggers. Once many beginners have tried out paddles, they're eager to try the flogger. Floggers consist of multiple strands of a long, string-like material attached to a handle. When swung, the tips of these strands should hit the designated target.

Floggers can feel like a massage or can inflict a significant amount of pain. It all depends on the way the flogger is made and how it is used. Heavier floggers are likely to create a massaging sensation, while lighter ones are likely to be a bit more painful. Soft materials, such as suede or faux fur, will offer a gentler feeling, while harsher materials, like unsoftened leather or rubber, will deliver a sharper strike with a lot more bite.

How to Use It

The flogger requires a coordinated motion of the wrist to allow the tips of the flogger's tails to touch an intended point on the receiver's body. This can include rolling the wrist, a gentle back and forth motion, and many other gestures. It's imperative you practice these movements on inanimate objects before you move onto using them on a partner.

While it may look easy at first, aiming a flogger can be difficult, and you don't want to accidentally hit a bony part of the body. Start with a gentle flogger, such as one made from faux fur until you perfect your technique.

The Tickler

Ticklers are sensation-inducing items and are usually attached to the top of long rods so they can be used from a distance. Sensation-inducing items include soft suede strands, feathers, metal beads, rubber strands, and more. Ticklers can feel soft and gentle on the skin—and usually leads to tickling and laughing. When used a bit more roughly, ticklers can leave a stinging sensation and leave marks on the skin.

How to Use It

To use a tickler for tickling, use a light hand and run the tickler softly across your partner's skin. Try to choose areas that are more sensitive for better results. While ticklers are primarily used for tickling, these small, portable items can be used for impact play as well. Instead of using the tickler in a dragging motion, use it in more of a spanking fashion.

Be careful not to touch sensitive areas like eyes or ears. You don't want the fibers to end up irritating the body. Stick to large, fleshy areas. Start with soft gentle tickles with your tickler and then mix in a light tap with the plastic of the tickler rod. Try several types and get your partner to choose which one he wants, then touch his skin with the different ones.

The Riding Crop

The riding crop is mostly used in equestrian sports as an encouragement tool and are long, flexible rods with a unique tip at the end. It's a mixture of a cane and a paddle. The tip of a riding crop produces the most sensation. Depending on how much force is put behind the strike, it can feel particularly painful—or it can feel like a gentle tap. The amount of force behind the strike makes a huge difference. Light taps and lightly touching the skin can be teasing, while direct taps can produce more pain.

How to Use It

To produce the two different sensations, you'll need to strike the skin with different forces. To be softer, just use the tip gently, but to produce more pain, then a more forceful strike will create a very painful sensation. Alternatively, you can use the flexible rod of the riding crop much like you'd use a cane. Be aware that many riding crops can feel as intense as a cane when used in this manner.

CHAPTER 22
Basics of a Great Spanking

The basics of spanking involve establishing consent, creating an agreement, planning the event, preparing costumes, tools and the scene, then allowing it to unfold in a safe, sexy, and fun way. The actual act of spanking is striking your man for the sexual arousal or gratification for both of you. It may involve very light and brief spanking or a much more extensive session, including the use of implements, such as whips or paddles.

Activities range from a spontaneous smack on bare buttocks during sexual activity to occasional sexual role-play, such as age-play or domestic discipline and may involve the use of a hand or other tools, such as a spanking paddle or cane. The paddle is the tool used to strike your partner on the buttocks. The act of spanking a person with a paddle is known as "paddling."

When we refer to dominance and submission in BDSM, we're talking about consensual power exchange. Meaning that even if your man, a submissive partner, is tied up and allows the dominant partner, the Queen, to dictate what happens, the terms have been discussed and agreed upon by both beforehand. Respect your man's limits. Before trying anything new, talk it over with him to make sure you're both into whatever is about to happen. Communication is part of having good sex. The willingness to talk about the kind of sex we have or want to have is a key skill.

Kate McCombs, a sex and relationships educator, states, "When you avoid those vital conversations, you might avoid some awkwardness, but you're also settling for suboptimal sex." By having these conversations, you and your partner's relationship can have emotional, psychological, and mental benefits. Sexual likes and dislikes can run on a spectrum. There are activities you love, ones you can't even think about, and all the stuff in between. And what happens to things that you haven't even heard of yet? Or when your Queen desires change? Communicating such intimate needs requires a high-level of confidence and trust. At the same time, communication builds confidence and trust. Think about what you would be comfortable with and what makes you uncomfortable.

Communicating these needs with your partner helps keep things open. Femdom can be virtually new and unfamiliar territory. Buried emotions can emerge, so discussing how you and your man feel about adding spanking to your sex lives — as well as brainstorming any unforeseen consequences and how you will deal with them — is important.

Femdom activities are commonly combined with other forms of sexual foreplay. All acts must be consensual, and the scene should be pre-negotiated. It's pivotal to establish a safe word that stops play if needed. For instance, "yellow" is often used to mean "slow down" and "red" to mean "stop." Adhering to the safe word and respecting it is crucial.

Learning each other's turn ons and boundaries are all part of the fun of BDSM.

During spanking, it's also important to only hit fleshy areas with a good amount of fat and muscle. So, when spanking, you should focus on the meatiest part of your partner's behind. Try to go as low as you can without hitting the leg. It is important to go low in order to be able to stimulate the genital region successfully with every hit. Use your partner's reactions to find out if it's working and to what extent. You will have to use the same principle to find the perfect amount of force used. Unless he directly demands it, don't ever spank so hard that you leave a trace. Another important thing to remember is to remove any jewelry you might have because it can cause unwanted injuries.

It is best to increase blood flow to an area to make it really sensitive and as pleasurable as possible, so a feather tickler is a great way to create that pins-and-needles type feeling across someone's skin. They'll then be sensitive to kisses and licks and tickles, and all the things that follow.

Begin very slow to get feedback all along. How is he doing? Is he enjoying it? Is it too much? The Queen should start with the hand, then move to other tools, like the paddle or flogger. It is imperative to be cognizant if your partner is enjoying it. If you're in a relationship, you can initiate discussions early on about spanking and raise the idea of trying it before actually doing it. If you're dating someone casually, it is important to figure out if it's something you want to engage in early on. Ensure you have consent — even if you have been married for a long time. Consent means the ability to stop a sexual encounter at any moment, including changing their mind.

Dr. Dulcinea Pitagora, also known as the "King Doctor," is a licensed psychotherapist and sex therapist who focuses on providing affirmative, sex-positive therapy to those with atypical sexual and gender expressions. Dr. Pitagora has also been a member of the NYC kink scene for more than a decade and formerly worked as a professional dominatrix. She defines sexual spanking as performed in the context of a role-play. The reality is that no one is getting punished for anything. It's part of a scene that you've already negotiated. The goal is mutual pleasure. You're experiencing it because the person doing the spanking enjoys spanking, and the person being spanked likes to be spanked.

In Femdom, couples will take it a little further. The importance of male obedience in this relationship cannot be overstated, so many couples enjoy using spanking as punishment, and some Queens will spank a man to tears. Men admit to being turned on when he submits completely to this degree of spanking. When a man submits, he is also admitting that he respects his woman and her decisions. He knows that when he is punished, it is never out of anger but out of love from the Queen. All men are not the same, and some men can take a lot while others will cry with barely any swats administered.

In the Female Led Relationship, the Queen rules and administers the spanking. Once there is consent, she decides how much and when to stop — unless the man uses his safe word.

Spanking can bring out a man's submissive side and break down his resistance and shame from being in a vulnerable position, naked over his Queen's lap, being spanked. Spanking is part of a man's submission, and when he submits to such an obviously painful and humbling experience, he will behave better and his attitude toward the Queen is greatly improved—not because he is fearful of the spanking but out of respect and the knowledge that his Queen is now more powerful than he is, and she will protect him from himself and his bad actions.

Giving discipline to a misbehaving man is not cruelty, it is love. And in a Female Led Relationship, the more you teach a man to behave properly, the more loving ensues. The Queen must take the lead in discussions and in administering the act. It is essential that the Queen respects how much her man is willing to take and how long it takes him to fully commit. Both partners should take time to warm up. So, add in spanking gradually. Spanking should be an appetizer, not the main course.

In a Femdom, the Queen may decide to spank first where she is in control, followed by oral sex where her man takes over and finally intercourse. As the submissive, and loyal servant knight of the Queen, her man is expected to follow her lead. If she wants to use the tickler before the cane, then this is her decision, and within the limits of how much her man can take.

As the leader of the *Love & Obey* movement, I have seen how spanking and discipline can transform couples and their sex lives. I know women are superior and must have complete and absolute obedience from men. I believe discipline helps men recognize female authority over them and creates submission. Men must be taught to be obedient and submissive to women.

CHAPTER 23
Best Positions for Spanking

S panking positions will vary according to the physical attributes of the Queen and her man. If she is tall and strong, she may prefer different positions and may use various tactics than a smaller and weaker woman. Physicality on its own will not determine the Queen's desire to try all positions, just some may be more comfortable. I encourage you both to try it all and see what works. Variety is the spice of life, so don't be afraid to add your own modifications.

Best Spanking Positions:

1. Standing

There is no positioning involved. The Queen simply approaches her man from behind and hits his bottom. This is used mostly for impromptu, short spankings to deliver a quick warning to him, which works well for punishment or discipline in an ongoing dominant/submissive relationship. However, most people do not like to be surprised with a spanking, so doing this needs to be negotiated beforehand.

If consensual, the surprise factor creates vulnerability and embarrassment. Pain is also higher when you are unprepared for it. Sometimes the Queen can spank her man in passing as a fun little surprise tap. I always suggest that if your man disrespects you or misbehaves, a little spanking on his butt while around the house does wonders. First, it reminds him of who is in charge, and second, it helps to address the issue without getting too serious.

This is an interesting position for role-playing, which sets the mood. You are the headmistress, and he has been a bad schoolboy. Or he is the criminal, and you are the naughty police officer. Maybe he needs to be up against a wall and spread 'em. Don't underestimate the power of teasing.

2. Bound and Blindfolded

If your man is bound and blindfolded, everything is a surprise, and he has no idea what's coming next. I always suggest lying face up, sitting up, or standing. Never place a man face down as it could affect his breathing. The blindfold is the element of surprise whether you're going to go hard or soft, fast or slow. He also can't see what instrument you're going to use, so feel free to play. It's also fun to watch them tense up when they feel nothing but the breeze coming from a paddle you might be waving near the target area, or they hear the swoosh of a cane as you flick it through the air.

Adding sensory deprivation to your sex life is an easy and tantalizing way to build tension. When you temporarily subtract stimuli from one sense, you can heighten others. For instance, when you can't see because you're wearing a blindfold, a whisper in your ear or the taste of your partner's mouth may seem all the more intense — and exciting.

If you want to buy a blindfold, start with a comfy silk scarf. You can also use a sleeping mask or the silk tie of a bathrobe. Depending on what role you want to play, ask your partner to blindfold you or ask if you can blindfold them. Once the blindfold is on, the partner can tease and tantalize the wearer, leaving them guessing what's coming next by kissing all over their body, whispering dirty talk into their ear, or tickling erogenous zones with a feather.

3. Bent Over Furniture

The Queen can stand in this act, but the man is bent over a desk, a table, or the back of an armchair. Alternatively, he is made to kneel over the edge of the bed, over a chair, or to kneel on a chair. In public play spaces, spanking benches are specially created for this position. With most furniture, the Queen can press her left (non-dominant) hand over the lower back of her man to add a bit of restraint. Being bent over a piece of furniture is mildly embarrassing.

In this position, there is lots of room to swing the arm and the Queen can really put her weight into it to gain more force. This position is very comfortable for your man. The main drawback is that there is no physical contact with the Queen's body, creating an emotional distance.

4. Over the Lap

This is the classical spanking position. The Queen sits on a chair or on the edge of the bed, and the man is face down over her lap. He is over the Queen's thighs and in contact with her lower belly. The great attributes about this position are the psychological effect of the mental image it creates, the contact with the Queen's body, and the fact that the butt is lifted and exposed in all its beautiful roundness.

The main drawback of this position is that it is not a comfortable position for the man if he is large and heavy since he will tend to roll off the lap. Also, the Queen finds it easier to hit the buttock that is farthest from his belly, creating an uneven spanking. He can mimic a similar position lying face down on a sofa while the Queen is on a chair.

5. Over the Knee

The "over the knee" position is where the man lies on the Queen's leg with his hands and feet on the floor. This position can also be done if the Queen sits on a bed, preferably with her back supported by the head of the bed. This way, the man can rest his full body on the bed, which is more relaxing and stable. On a bed, the man can be moved away from the lap and onto the knees proper; this way, his bottom is farther from the Queen's body, who can now hit both buttocks more evenly. This is a great position for long spankings because it is comfortable and effortless for both the Queen and her man and has more body contact than bending over furniture.

However, the man has to turn his head sideways to breathe. It is less embarrassing than other positions and only moderately vulnerable. Another drawback is that there is no restraint, and a feisty man can struggle and move around with ease. Restraint can be increased by holding his hand over his lower back, or by using bondage. This is a very sexy position as he is automatically in a position of weakness. As a woman, you can now go to town with your flogger or paddle, and he must lie there and take it. This can be very arousing for men. For added intensity, bound his hands together, then get him over your legs.

A variation of this that I personally love is lying on a coffee table. Feel free to tie his hands to the table on a cushion to support his penis. Now you have ample ability to use any tool. Sometimes I like to tie up my partner and leave him there to contemplate his bad behavior, then I return to administer punishment.

6. Straddling the Leg

This is a variant of the "over the lap" position that is very popular with the domestic discipline crowd. The man is made to straddle his Queen's thigh who is sitting on a chair or on the edge of the bed. Then the man leans forward and is held in position with the Queen's left arm. Holding one hand of the man on his lower back and wrapping the right leg of the Queen over the man's left calf can restrain her almost completely. This is quite an embarrassing and vulnerable position because it spreads the legs, exposing the anus.

If it's a woman experiencing this, her clit will be stimulated during the spanking, creating a deeply sexual experience. This is a great position to spank a woman to orgasm. Cumming while being spanked is quite a mental trip. If it's the man, the effects on his cock and balls can vary from pleasurable to painful. In any case, the body contact is great, the restraint is nice, and the Queen can hit both buttocks forcefully and evenly. Lack of back support for the Queen may be a main problem, but this can be solved by sitting in an armchair.

7. Man Table

This position can be easily created with the man kneeling on all fours like a table. The Queen sits on the sofa and can be bent over. This position is great because the Queen is free to move around as she pleases. She can place her feet up on his back for added fun.

The drawback for "man table" is that if your man has a back problem, then it could be uncomfortable.

8. Sitting on or Straddling the Man

The wrestling spanking is a fun game in which the man does not submit to the spanking but has to be wrestled and immobilized by the Queen. This may also require that the man is immobilized throughout the spanking so that he cannot escape. One way to achieve this is to sit straddling his lower back. To get away, the man would need to pull up his weight and that of the Queen, which for most people is impossible.

It is also difficult for him to turn over or to protect his bottom with his hands, because the Queen's body blocks the way. Hence, the man has to endure his punishment until the

Queen decides to stop, which makes for high vulnerability and embarrassment. The main problem is that a heavy Queen may injure the man's back, therefore, this needs to be given careful consideration. Otherwise, it is a very domineering position for a spanking.

9. Wheelbarrow Position

This is the most exposed and humiliating position for a spanking. The Queen sits on a sofa or an armchair and the man places his legs up around her hips. His hands are on the floor, and he is balanced with his hips up. The buttocks can now be spanked like playing a drum. If the Queen desires, she can have her man hold this position for quite a while. This can be great for a very athletic man but much harder for one who is not as strong. The turn on is that this is a vulnerable position so the man with his butt in the air can be stimulated. This position would be great for shorter positions.

CHAPTER 24
Femdom and Bondage

F emdom involves BDSM of which bondage is the first part. Bondage is the practice of consensually tying, binding, or restraining a partner for erotic, aesthetic, or somatosensory stimulation. In Femdom, you may be physically restrained in a variety of ways, including the use of rope, cuffs, bondage tape, or self-adhering bandage. Sexuality and erotica are an important aspect in bondage but are often not the end in itself. Aesthetics also play an important role in bondage.

A common reason for her to tie you up is so you both can up gain pleasure from the restraint. She will exercise her feeling of control and domination over you, and you will feel complete submission and transfer of control and power to her. For sadomasochistic people, bondage is often used as a means to an end, where the restrained partner is more accessible to other sadomasochistic behavior. However, bondage can also be used alone to create that sensual pleasure from the feeling of vulnerability and your Queen can feel complete dominance both of which are very erotic.

Many couples in Female Led Relationships and those exploring Femdom incorporate bondage into their sex lives. This sometimes takes the form of a sex game or sexual fantasy enactment. Bedroom bondage games may be used for sexual arousal or as a form of foreplay that requires and implies a level of trust and a surrender of control. The main feature of sexual bondage is that it renders the restrained person vulnerable to a variety of sex acts, including some that they may be inhibited from otherwise engaging. The restrained partner is dependent for their sexual satisfaction on the actions of their partner, who may treat the restrained partner as their sex object.

What occurs next is simply fun, playful, sensual and erotic. Bedroom bondage is usually mild, with one partner voluntarily being put into restraints by being tied up or handcuffed. It may involve simple hand ties, bed restraints, being tied to a chair, etc. Blindfolds are a common part of bedroom play. The restrained partner may then be sexually stimulated by masturbation, fingering, hand job, oral sex, a vibrator, intercourse, or other sex acts. Bondage can also be used for purposes other than sexual foreplay, for example, it may be used in erotic tickling or for sexual teasing. It's all about acting out sexual fantasies.

CHAPTER 25
Femdom and Role-Playing

R ole-play during sex involves acting out a sexual fantasy, which helps couples to transition into Femdom activities easier. Role-playing may be done during foreplay or can be the main event. According to the 2015 Sexual Exploration in America Study, more than 22 percent of sexually active adults engage in role-playing. Couples love role-play to spice things up and try new things or be someone else. Femdom is made so much more intense when you and your Queen have specific roles you want to play and scenes you want to enact. The concept of creating rituals can also be added to role-play to make things even more formal.

This tends to be sexually arousing because suddenly you and your Queen can perform elaborate acts out of the norm. Femdom presents a perfect time to use role-play because the Queen becomes a character who is in complete control. Each role adds to the power dynamic of dominance and submission. Some couples become so involved in role-play they insist on elaborate costumes and scripts. Many fetish parties will act out role-playing fantasies to make the scene more exciting and thrilling.

Nearly any role could become the base material for an erotic experience, and there is no limit to what objects an individual could consider sexual. It may, for example, involve wearing a costume that is regarded as erotic, such as a miniskirt and stockings, or one or both partners being nude, say for an evening. It may involve elements of dominance and submission, passivity, or obedience. It may involve sexual bondage, with either partner being restrained. Bondage plus spanking go together perfectly.

Another element that makes sexual role-play appealing is that the concept of it not just about the physical act of getting off. It's just as stimulating for the mind as it is for the body.

When the Queen and her man can truly let go to fulfill their deepest fantasies in the form of role-playing, it taps right into the imagination, creating an even sexier physical experience.

Exciting Role-Playing Games Include:

1. Doctor or nurse and Patient

2. Teacher and Student

3. Escort and Client

4. Boss and Employee

5. Housewife and Handyman (Plumber or Carpenter)

6. Master and Slave

7. Photographer and Model: this allows one partner to photograph the other as a precursor to sexual interaction

8. Female Villain and James Bond

9. CIA Agent and Criminal

10. Strangers in a bar

The best way to start something new is to discuss it with your partner, so you are both excited about it and can come up with fantasies that will stimulate both of you. You want to ensure you are both comfortable and willing to add it to your sex life. Not everyone likes to add new things to sex. Many people are quite happy with normal, so it is important to ensure both of you are eager. As the Queen in a Female Led Relationship, this may be something you wish to add to your sex sessions and your man is obligated to follow your lead. But it is important to respect his ideas as well. If it is the man who must convince the Queen, be respectful and make your suggestions but allow her to make the final decision. This is why communication becomes extremely important.

Role-playing doesn't need to be complicated. You can start out with doing some smaller and simpler things to get each other going. This could be wearing lingerie or trying out a sex toy. Heck, the two of you could even test out by speaking with accents or using different props. Start simple and then move to complicated. Once you have done it a few times, you can create more complicated scenarios. This is the point when you can add spanking and combine the two. Remember, role-play should be fun. It may feel awkward and intimidating at first, but it's worth trying it out. The best way to figure out what works for you and your man is simply to try it out.

CHAPTER 26
The Perfect Femdom Playroom

One of the greatest ways to make your Femdom and sex sessions so much more exciting is to set up a playroom—*Fifty Shades of Grey* style. There is a reason we were so excited when Christian Grey led Ana into the most luxurious playroom. A sex playroom becomes a very special place for better sex, more relaxation, and a greater connection with your partner. A Queen can really feel like royalty in a playroom.

A playroom can enhance the sexiness of your sex and Femdom play. Your playroom can have every type of equipment for play artistically laid out, resembling a kinky hotel room in Las Vegas. A bench with restraints, the cross, even a swing contraption has been used. The whips can range from a very sturdy paddle or leather flogger and whips. Some couples get into monogrammed restraints and very creative garb. Who can forget the capes and grand halls of a mansion in *Eyes Wide Shut*? You and your Queen can wear sumptuous capes or luxurious monogrammed robes until the fun begins. You can use masks or any other type of costumes you enjoy.

Red and black are the most popular colors or something regal with rich purples, yellows, and blues. Lighting doesn't need to be dark, but it can be. Soft and romantic, harsh spotlights, or disco balls can create a fun scene. Some couples create shrines and other formal areas in their homes for Queen worship. It's essential to make your sex life and exciting time of exploration and fantasy. The ideas for you to take your sex life to a whole new level of excitement and arousal are endless.

Great Sex Dungeon Toys, Accessories, and Furniture:

Sex Swing. A sex swing is such a great addition to a dungeon, and you don't have to fasten it to the ceiling with a large screw. There are some that are built to fit on a door jamb and are versatile enough to accommodate several different positions.

Blackout Mask. If you are not able to fully black out your windows, a blackout mask is a great way to create atmosphere and suspense. It's a great feature to keep hanging on your dungeon wall.

Cuffs. A dungeon wouldn't be complete without having a set of handcuffs on hand to restrain your partner. You can keep your cuffs near a bed. You can also place your partner's wrists above their head. Better yet — if you are doing some bed play or even floor play, suction cuffs are an awesome option for restraint.

Collar and Leash. Your bottom/submissive might like to be led around by the collar in a session. In that case, you can install a hook on the wall and hang a collar and leash to use in your dungeon.

Spanking Paddle. Tools for pain play can be a big part of your dungeon play. There are so many to choose from, from whips to floggers to canes.

Bondage Rope. Bondage should be done with high quality rope that will not fray or leave marks. There are many variations you can find online but make sure to choose only high-quality rope made specifically for this type of activity.

Strap-On. If you and your Queen want to get into pegging, then choosing the right strap-on is key. You and your Queen should choose one made of high-quality materials and the right size for you. This decision should be made with input from both of you, so you are both prepared for the experience.

Knee Pads. You will want to protect your knees and having knee pads or a variety of cushions will help save your knees for when you want to show your devotion in this way.

Storage. Choosing the right storage is important so you can have easy access to your tools and store them away carefully. One way to organize and store your tools when not using them is to install hooks on the walls of your dungeon. This not only helps keep you organized but having them out on display can set the psychological tone you may want for your submissive.

Fun Furniture You Can Add:

Spanking Bench. The spanking bench, or spanking horse, is a piece of furniture used to position your man on it, with or without restraints. Even celebrities like Cara Delevingne and Ashley Benson have reported buying and using a sex bench.

Cara has previously hinted at an interest in BDSM during an interview on RuPaul's podcast *RuPaul: What's the Tee?* The spanking bench is similar to a sawhorse with a padded top and rings for restraints.

What's nice about it is that it allows the Queen to move around her subject easily, choosing to taunt and tease him from any angle. With restraints, it will ensure your man is held in place and he is comfortable. Some couples have these custom-made with luxurious materials or just high-quality leather. It creates the ability to explore a multitude of sexual positions, and it can also be easily folded up and stored away since it is also designed to be discreet.

Sex Couch. A sex couch is the ultimate, classic sex lounge chair. It's designed so you can sit on it in a variety of ways to achieve that perfect position. Many come with straps and extra pillows to prop yourself up further or to have bondage furniture.

BDSM Bondage Board. Bondage frame boards and tables are adjustable so you can strap or rope a person to the board. This table has convenient holes with access points for the face, nipples, and genitals, and it is collapsible, so you can store it under the bed or in a closet. It makes for a great addition to any playroom.

Queening Stool. Queening stool is a great addition which makes it more comfortable for when you and your Queen are doing facesitting. It's safer for your Queen to sit above you so she avoids accidentally smothering you. It will also help to ease tension on her legs and back, since it can be a challenge to remain in the position for an extended period.

Bondage Cross. A bondage cross is a standing fixture that allows you to strap someone in a vertical position. It's a stark fixture for your burgeoning sex dungeon or a very interesting, abstract sculpture in the living room that your Uncle Joe might ask about sometime. The cross above is designed with vinyl upholstery and hand-welded aluminum, so you're getting the top-of-the-line as far as bondage furniture is concerned. Choose furniture that is high-quality and well made, even if it's just one or two pieces. Make sure floors, walls, furniture, and other surfaces are easily cleaned and sanitized.

If you're going to use candles for wax play or decoration, nearby fabrics should be flame retardant. Battery candles can be convincing enough if you want mood lighting without worrying about the fire department showing up. Carpeted floors might not be the best idea, especially if you're going to be dealing with sweat, drool, and other bodily functions. Area rugs are the go-to if you really want something soft under your feet. Wood items should be sanded to avoid splinters. It's important to keep your playroom safe, warm, comfortable, and clean.

CHAPTER 27
Aftercare in Femdom

F emdom sessions are extremely intimate, requiring a huge level of trust and communication to experience intense play scenes. So, here's a guide to aftercare which should be a common routine practice in Femdom play.

Aftercare is an extremely important part of Femdom. Aftercare should always be present as a healthy part of any BDSM dynamic. You and your Queen are human and will need a little taking care of when your limits and boundaries have been pushed to the extreme. Aftercare is the act of checking in after a play session. It is built into the Dom/Sub routine as a way to ensure everyone feels safe and comfortable.

Aftercare can be entirely what you and your Queen decide. It often consists of relaxing and winding down after sex, which could include hugging, talking, taking a hot bath or shower, rubbing lotion on any bruises or marks or a massage to sore areas. For some, aftercare could be sitting on the sofa together or going for a walk. You and your Queen will want to discuss how you're feeling. It is important to have a light discussion about how the session went, what went well, and what could have been omitted. Be honest and keep the conversation open and constructive.

This is a great time for you both to learn how to improve the sessions. Feel free to add some treats, water, chocolate, tea, aloe vera, or muscle cream. Sometimes there may be an emotional release. Allow these things to happen naturally. The more open the discussion, the better your sessions. Aftercare isn't just for the physical wounds that may be acquired during a BDSM scene but is about psychological well-being too. The purpose of aftercare is to give you and your Queen a chance to reflect on the play session, talk about what you each liked and disliked, and discuss worries or concerns. This can also strengthen your bond with each other.

Things to Do

- Communicate before, during, and after.

- Practice with your tools beforehand.

- Test your toys and tools on yourself to learn their intensity.

- Choose a safety word.

- Watch body language.

- Deliver aftercare.

- Have a medical kit readily available.

How to Improve Communication

1. **Learn to be calm and relaxed.** If a conversation is making you angry, anxious, or frustrated, learning to self-soothe is key. If you respond from an angry place, or if you are anxious, nervous, or scared, you are likely to say words you don't mean, things that are hurtful, point blame, and/or criticize. Practice breathing. Take long deep breaths and count to ten. Go outside for some fresh air. It's okay to say, "I will be right back, I need a break." Practice breathing often, not just during a heated conversation, but while driving, while at your desk, even while relaxing. Breathing is at the core of becoming calm. And the absolute best time to talk is when you are calm.

2. **Be nonjudgmental.** Shut off your critical and emotional mind and really listen to what your partner is saying. Empathize by putting yourself in your partner's shoes, if you need to.

3. **Use positive language.** This is also about remembering to avoid blaming, pointing the finger, criticizing, and judging. Instead, reveal your feelings. For example, instead of saying, "You don't even try to please me," try this: "I really feel unsatisfied with our lovemaking these days." Focus on using "I feel" and avoid using "you" in the sentence.

4. **Listen.** Summarize, paraphrase, or repeat what your partner has said. This is an easy way to let your partner know you have heard them and can often diffuse an angry situation. If your partner says, "I am angry and sexually frustrated these days, and you don't seem to

care about sex." Instead of responding defensively, which might be your inkling, this is a great opportunity for you to make the conversation productive. You can respond by saying, "It sounds like you are feeling dissatisfied with our sex life. Perhaps we could find a solution."

5. **Touch while talking.** Holding your partner's hand or putting your hand on his/her knee can remind you and your partner that you are on his/her side, and that you two are in this together. It promotes intimacy.

6. **Compliment.** Compliments are a big part of positive talk. It's essential for our partners to feel recognized and appreciated. I recommend a minimum of three compliments a day. The best way to catch a bee is with sugar.

CHAPTER 28
Spice Up Your Femdom Sex Life

Thirty Great Tips for Spicing Up Your Overall Sex Life:

1. **Have an affair with your Queen**. Plan your date and pretend you're both having an affair with each other. Seduce each other, tease, and be sexy and adventurous.

2. **Bed roles.** Dressing like another human is an easy way for all your secret desires to be achieved without an affair. Try to be a physician, patient, teacher, student, or even a soldier.

3. **Think like a kid.** As a young teenager, you may have fallen in love. But that doesn't mean now and then you shouldn't behave like one. Make yourself creative and act like you're 18 years old on the weekend. Dress like one, hang out, and become a teenager.

4. **Focus on Foreplay.** The emphasis on foreplay is one of the best ways to have great sex. Only spend fifteen more minutes getting horny before having sex. You're

both going to have better sex finally. During those fifteen minutes, caress and praise one another's body.

5. **Make sex unforeseen and unforeseeable.** No matter how complicated it might seem, avoid planning sex or programming sex unless you are both busy.

7. **Be innovative and shockingly fair.** As the relationship matures, new ways to become creative must be built. Treat yourself to something that makes your heart race and your sex life super sexy.

8. **Get your bed sexy stuff**. Bring your bed with fresh anticipation. Visit your nearest pharmacy or an adult shop and expose your senses to sex toys, lubricants, pheromones, and everything else.

9. **Feel sexy**. Look cute, and if you have to, continue to work out. Give yourself a sweet look, wear sexy lingerie, and get a new haircut for yourself. Feel sexy, and you're going to look sexy.

10. **Live the dreams of your wildest ones**. Just because you have a long-term relationship does not mean you shouldn't embrace your fantasies. Talk to your friend about it and enjoy it together.

11. **Practice withdrawal.** It'll lose its charm if you know you can have sex whenever you want. Stop having sex every now and then— and save it for days if you go clubbing or relax a bit. Plan this right, and it could be an enormous turn on.

12. **Shock factor.** Sexually shock one another. Surprise your partner occasionally into a sexual high. Surprise him when he comes home naked or tell him that when

both of you come out to dinner, you're not wearing your panties under your short skirt.

13. **Think beyond the bed.** Think beyond the bed. In addition to the bed, there are many attractive areas. Think of a kitchen, couch, toilet, patio, or swimming pool. Get creative, and it will be more fun to reward people.

14. **Add Food.** Fill the mood with food and drinks. Give meals or cook together. Aphrodisiac food will make your love more romantic and make you horny with a few drinks.

15. **Massages with sensuality**. Get naked and give one another a sex-free sensual massage. Seek pleasure and encourage your fingers to linger for a while. As long as your partner's orgasm is focused on, it will make you both feel good.

16. **Try tantric Sex.** Bring tantric sex into the bedroom for an intense and passionate sexual encounter.

17. **Think kinky.** There is nothing to remove the thrill of wild sex when the relationship starts to slow down in bed. Discuss your dreams and give life to your fetishes and extravagant wishes.

18. **Take a fun vacation from time to time.** Choose a holiday destination that you both want, whether it's a crowded sex resort or a lovely idyllic paradise island. So, spend all your holidays just dreaming of sexy feelings.

19. **Calling and sending hot emails**. Don't wait until you seduce your partner. Just send a few sexy pictures in

the middle of the day and taunt your partner if you both want to meet at night.

20. **Watch porn.** Sometimes watching porn helps both of you to get in the mood and make love better by watching a couple on the screen.

21. **Fool around**. Do not try to tie yourself up with each other for any time alone. Be loving to each other all the time and sometimes take affection to an entirely new level. If they are on the phone, take their pants off and give them an oral call in the middle of a phone call.

22. **Body play**. Instead of having sex, play with each other's bodies. Paint with glow-in-the-dark or edible colors on your partner's body.

23. **Make a video from home**. Create a video while you have sex together. Delete it, if you make a sex tape or hide it in a secure place after the act has been done. Watching you age in the video and concurrently can be a massive rush for everyone.

24. **Wear revealing clothing.** Show something, and make it look like an accident, every now and then.

25. **Using mirrors.** Use full-length mirrors to increase your sexual experience alongside your bed. When you want to recreate a foursome romantic dream, you can have sex very close to the mirror. See or imagine a new pair of yourself.

26. **Make a little bit of noise.** Moaning or whispering sexy nothings in bed is an enormous turn on that cannot be explained. Speak in bed, and in no time, you're going to wake up your partner.

27. **Sexual configuration**. Give your room a glimpse of sex. Use perfumes and candles to make lovemaking feel like a luxurious luxury.

28. **Be real.** You cannot enjoy or even be faithful to the best sex in your life until you both share thoughts and sexual memories, whether it be about a romantic obsession or a sentimental memory, with each other. Avoid being mentally awkward, and your sex relationship will flourish.

29. **Read an erotic novel together.** The spirit is our most significant sexual organ. Build and envision dreams. It's going to be a more substantial turn than you think.

30. **Creating sexual memory.** Always try something new. Having sex in a car or on a beach during a holiday, swimming nude in a pool, or even as a couple in bed. So as long as you both continuously make fresh and exciting memories, sex will never get boring.

31. **Be faithful to the relationship.** Notwithstanding love and trust in the air, nothing can tarnish your relationship than unfaithfulness. You may go so far as to swing or engage in other kinky ideas. But as long as there is love and confidence, you can find a way to rekindle the sexual excitement without getting lost. You will probably stand the test of time if you're looking for opportunities to have better sex with your partner. Enjoy the bliss of romance and keep your passion boiling together with new and sexy things.

Conclusion

There is no doubt that Femdom is growing, and it shows no signs of slowing down. More couples want to experiment and explore concepts of domination and submission and are getting into BDSM. BDSM is a variety of erotic practices involving bondage, discipline dominance, submission, and sadomasochism. BDSM involves one partner being submissive and the other being dominant. Female domination involves the Queen as the dominant and taking control, while you are the submissive and submit to her.

Femdom is the more intense version of a Female Led Relationship. Most couples start out in FLR with moderate aspects of female domination, such as the Queen taking charge of the household, making the major decisions, giving the orders and being in control in the bedroom. Female Led Relationships are much more focused on day-to-day interactions where the Queen is in charge in the relationship and her man serves her as the supportive gentleman.

However, after some time of being in an FLR, many couples want to increase the intensity of domination and submission, especially in the bedroom. In Femdom, it is important that exploration be done together. Keep it fun and safe. The use of negotiations for limits and boundaries are mandatory along with safe words. You want to use Femdom to form a deeper connection with your Queen and make your relationship or marriage much more exciting and filled with adventure. It is important to have deep discussions about your fantasies and desires but be open to what you may learn.

Femdom is also a way for you to improve your servitude to your Queen. Preparing for your Femdom sex sessions is crucial and adding sexual additions like furniture, toys, and costumes will only make the experience even more thrilling. Though Femdom may include activities with a basis in BDSM, exploring these activities as a way to spice up your Female Led Relationship is perfectly acceptable and encouraged.

You and your Queen's commitment to your primary relationship is key. It is my hope that Femdom and many other ideas I share in my *Love & Obey* series serve to help you have more fun, adventure, and sexual fulfillment than you ever thought possible. The *Love & Obey* movement supports female empowerment, and your commitment to the lifestyle will truly bring you and your Queen the happiness you deserve.

Printed in Great Britain
by Amazon

79230108R00096